Here is how it all happened: It started almost a year ago, February 15th, 2014. My sister, Annie was on Google looking for contact information regarding my estranged sons Billy and Todd. Instead, she found my ex-wife Elaine. This was after 30+ years of no communication with her. She called Elaine, and found out she's now living in Sun City, Arizona. Both were surprised by the time that had passed. They soon caught up and began talking like lost old friends, and must have chatted for over an hour. Annie called me and mentioned her call with Elaine.

"That's nice," I responded, then asked how she was doing.

"Really good," she said, "you should call her and say hi one of these days."

It's been over 12 years since we last talked. What do you say, after so long?

"Maybe, I don't know." I reminded her, "It's been 30 years since we've been divorced, 12 years since we even talked on the phone. It didn't go so well."

"You know she had breast cancer," Annie remarked. "She's doing well, no more cancer." She sounded like a real sweetie; you should give her a call."

"The past is the past," I said, bringing an end to the topic, "I'll have to think on it."

Several months passed, and Annie calls Elaine and they have another nice talk.

"She said she would really like to hear from you," Annie encouragingly says, "she sounds really nice, give her a call."

"Maybe I will." I didn't know what say other than that.

Time goes by again; it's December, nearing

Christmas of 2014. I call Annie, wishing her the

best of the Christmas season.

"Hi sis, are you doing any decorating for Christmas?"

"Oh yes, for sure. That's my fun time. Are you?"

"No, can't get in that Christmas spirit when you're a senior by yourself. It's just any other day."

, Annie brings Elaine up again.

"What's she doing for Christmas? Why don't you call her? You know she's all alone, too."

"Okay, sis, maybe I will."

But I don't, again. January 2015 comes and I'm thinking about Elaine. Her birthday is on the 21st and it's already the 19th. I mail her a little note, hoping she'll get it by the 21st, wishing her a happy birthday, with my phone number written on it. Surprisingly, she calls me and we talk about some old times since it's been a long time when we last talked. Our call lasts for about 20 minutes, and I

wrap it up, saying that it was nice to talk to her

again.

"Why don't you come and visit me? Stay a couple of days," adds Elaine.

"Sounds good. Maybe I will in a couple of weeks."

"I was just thinking," she continued, "maybe I could come up and get you this Saturday, in two days, and see Sedona."

"Let me think about it."

"Okay." She sounded sad on the other end.

"It's nice hearing from you," I continued, "we will talk again."

"Thanks for the birthday note."

I hang up, thinking about our call. It's been 30

years, her voice sounds a little older. It would be

nice to see her again, since we used to always get

along.

After 20 minutes, thinking about that call with her and about her coming up, I call her back.

"Hi, it's me. Are you sure you want to come up here and get me? It's 120 miles up here from Sun City."

"Yes," she reassured me, "I'm sure that it'll be a nice drive. I've always wanted to see Sedona."

"Okay, I'll give my directions when you pull into the Camp Verde turn off."

"Okay, see you Saturday."

We say our farewells, and as I sat, with my phone in my hand, thinking what just happened. What the hell, I thought, it will be nice to see each other, maybe have fun. I've been thinking of getting out of Cottonwood, so I could stay a couple days and see what happens.

After two days of anxious waiting, it's 7:00

a.m. on Saturday, January 24th. Elaine's on her way, so I have some coffee, watching some dog shows, thinking what the experience is going to be like, as I'm 71 and she's 66. After not seeing each other, we would have changed a lot, as she was only 36 and I was 41 when we were last together. That was three decades ago, time in which we don't know how the other changed. I've had two days to think about that time, and her. Will we have anything in common, or will we be completely different? We used to always have fun together, so we'll have to play it by ear, as they say. My cell rang, and I answered.

"Hi," she started, "I'm starting my way up. See you in a couple hours."

"Okay, Elaine. Be careful."

We hang up. I'm kind of nervous. In two hours I'll be seeing my ex-wife after 30 years. I shook my head. The last time we were with each other, we were in Hollywood, where we eventually grew apart.

We went in different directions after our divorce. Who knows why these things happen, but they do. At least we parted as friends.

After 30 years, we would get to see each other, as I was staying with her for several days. Who knows if it works out, we may or we may not like each other. Many thoughts like these were running through my head as she was on her way. I tried to keep myself busy through cleaning my place. Often I would look out one of the windows. It was a nice day in Cottonwood, and she would be here in two hours.

Around 9:00 a.m. I tried to watch TV, but my stomach was acting up, as if I was a teenager waiting for his date.

Here I am, 71 years old, looking at my watch every two minutes. I go out for a walk to make the time go by. I go down to the U-Sell lot to look at some used cars.  There is nothing there so I cross over Highway 89A, to look at cars in the Dodge dealership and walk all the way down to 6th Street. It was time for me to head back so I quickly walked back home. It was 8:45 a.m. when she should have been at the Camp Verde exit.  I greeted a couple of people and checked my phone often until I arrived home. Back inside, I wait for her to call. It's been two and a half hours since we last talked.

My brother Wally can make the trip in less than two hours. Something must have happened: she may have changed her mind and went back home or her car broke down, when my phone starts to ring.

"Hi," I said.

"Hi, it's me. There's no Camp Verde turn off. I'm at some place called Rim Rock." She sounded upset on the other end.

"You missed the turn off. As I said, there's only the Cottonwood turn off. You're not that far, come back two miles and you'll see it."

I relay to her the directions to take the Camp Verde, Cottonwood exit, turn right, and then after 15 minutes' drive, take a left at the Chase Bank and another left at the Auto Zone. I stay with her on the phone, and after I make sure she knows where she's going, we hang up, and I look at my watch as I stand by the window, watching and waiting.

*She should be pulling into view,* I think to myself, and on cue, her white PT Cruiser drives by. I'm out the door as she opens her car door. Compared to 30 years ago, the last time we saw each other, she looks like the same Elaine I knew, but a little older. I give a little wave and we hug each other briefly.

"How was your drive?" I asked.

"Okay, except for taking the wrong turn off."

We go inside my place and I give her a brief tour of my apartment.

"There's not much to show here."

"I'm hungry. Didn't have any breakfast before I left. Is there a place close by to eat?"

"Do you still like Mexican food?"

"Yes!"

We were out in 60 seconds as I carried my two suitcases to her car and hopped in. I showed her the way to Hacienda, a sit down restaurant in the immediate area.

We pull into the parking lot and get out. She looks great for 66, always looked and dressed nicely. We inside and are seated with our menus, after which we quickly order. I still don't know what to say to her at this point, but it'll be a good start to eat and get reacquainted with one another after so long.

"Well, how have you been all these years?" I begin the conversation, at last.

"Oh, it's been hard. In the last ten years, my mom, dad, and Aunt Ruth died, and I'm diagnosed with cancer. I just work, mostly."

Our food comes in time. That was an earful. I wonder what to say to all her bad news.

"Sorry to hear all of that happened to you," offering my condolences.

We eat breakfast, engaging in small talk. Elaine asks,

"So what have you been doing with yourself all these years?"

"Just being a senior, which is hard to believe I am now. I wonder where all of those years went."

"Yes, it's hard for me, too, and I'm working, still."

"Are you still doing computer work?" I ask.

"Yes, for almost forty years, and I hate it. I've been doing it for the last twelve years at the same place." Elaine seems reluctant to talk about it.

"It can't be that bad. What is it that you do on the computer?"

"I work with this real estate company. I don't want to talk about it, I really hate my job, but it pays the bills."

I continue to eat, thinking she's living in the naive world if she hates her job.

"How far is Sedona from here?" she asks, changing the subject.

"It's twenty miles."

"I've always wanted to see Sedona. All the girls at work have been there."

"Have you heard of Jerome?" I ask, "It's an artist town, full of hundreds of shops and was an old copper mining town. Let's go there first. It has great history, lots of things to see."

"Okay, that sounds fun. And it's only 11:00 a.m.; maybe we still can go see Sedona."

We finish breakfast and get back into her little Cruiser, then head up the mountain's curvy road, many other drivers having the same thought.

Halfway up the steep drive, a feeling came over me, as if we never parted in the first place.

"What a nice day for a ride," she said as I pointed out sights along the road as we got closer to Jerome, the slower drivers in front of us giving us a chance to spot specific things.

I point at an old building on the steep slope and said,

"That used to be a hospital down there."

"All the homes are very colorful and nice looking," she remarks.

"Yes," I started, "they say, back in the sixties, the California hippies took over Jerome and made it into an artist town, so we have to thank them for this great place that they started. You see that red rock resale shop? My friend owns it. We have to see if he's there. I've never seen so many tourists up here. We'll be lucky to find a parking place."

Jerome was packed with tourists and locals today.

I tell Elaine that I know a friend who makes

jewelry, and wanted to stop by and say hi to him.

Main Street was completely packed. We had to go

around a couple of times, when we lucked out. A

car was backing out, and we thanked the driver. I

tell her Saturdays are busy, what with the motorcycle club being here. If we looked at the license plates, we may see nearly every state represented. We try and continue to make small talk as we cross the street down a small slope to Richard's jewelry shop, which was busy.

We look around until I spot Richard's son, also named Richard, and I ask if his dad is here.

"Yeah, dad's in the back working on some jewelry," he said and then yells in the back, "Dad, Richard's here to see you."

So many Richard's in one building.

We offer our greetings, and I introduce Elaine, who looks around as we talk. I tell the senior Richard I stopped by his house and saw the two big trash bins, which made me wonder if he was moving.

"No," my friend began, "a real bad thing happened. The whole inside burned up. We lost almost everything, so we're redoing the inside. It's a mess, but we are okay and just dealing with it."

"Sorry to hear about your luck," I tell him with some sympathy.

"Thanks. We didn't get hurt, thank God."

"Yes, thank God."

Elaine asked him about a potential commission to make a cross in the future, but he was really busy, so we said our farewells and left. I told her about what happened to their house, and why he was so busy. Together we walked the streets of Jerome and went in several shops and saw a lot of great art.

"Let's go see if one of my good friends is at his shop," I say at one point.

"Okay, sounds good to me. This is a nice little town with a lot to see. I'd like to go in all these shops," she said.

"We'd be here 'til midnight if we did that."

We pass three long blocks, all lined with shops, until we head down a hill with a staircase built upon it, and go down to the Red Rock resale. At the counter the woman said,

"Hi folks, if you need any help, let me know."

"Oh," I began, "I was hoping Westley was here."

"Sorry, he's not here today. Do you want to leave a message?"

"Just wanted to say hi. I'm a good friend of the family. Tell him Richard Corey stopped in. Thank you."

I told Elaine that Westley originally ran a shop in Sedona, but now he has another business in Jerome. As we walked out, I saw two ladies with three dogs across the street.

"I have to give them my card."

"What? Why?" Elaine asked, caught off guard.

"I have a website for pet lovers." I handed Elaine one of my business cards. She waited as I crossed the street.

"Hi ladies. Who are your friends?" I indicated by motioning to their dogs, "I have a website for pet lovers," and handed them each a card.

"Check it out, thanks." I gave each of their dogs a pet before I headed back to Elaine.

"What's this about?" she asked when I was by her side again.

"Oh, it's one of my hobbies. I love all animals, especially dogs. They keep me busy in my so called golden years." It's difficult to say it, but we really are seniors. We smiled.

"Yes," she replied, "I can't believe I'm sixty-six."

"What about me? I'm seventy one!" I shake my head and we head back to Main Street. We look in more shops until it was nearly 3 in the afternoon.

"Maybe we should head to Sedona now," I suggest.

"Maybe we should head back to Sun City? I

don't like driving at night. I can see Sedona another day."

"Sounds good to me," I agree, and we go back to her car to go down to Cottonwood.

We pass the Steve Cory car lots on the way back to Sun City.

"I sure like this Verde Valley," she remarked. "How long how have you been living here?"

"Over twenty years. It's a nice place to live. I've met a lot of people after this long."

Both of us enjoy sightseeing when we can on the I-17 freeway to Sun City. Many diesel trucks passed around us. We continued to make small talk, while I wondered what she was thinking, and wondered if she was thinking along the same line as me.

We pass the Cordes Junction, a sign we were getting closer.

"So, how long have you been living in Sun City?"

"Twelve years with my aunt Ruth. I was helping her with her health issues and she helped me with my breast cancer."

"That must have been hard on both of you."

"It's been hard for the last ten with almost all of my family passing. It's still hard to talk about," her voice trembling. I quickly changed the subject.

"Look at all of those Saguaro cactus. They've been here longer than the Indians."

We pass the Anthem shopping center down, then down a steep mountain way, passing Black Canyon City. What to say? Small talk potentially could turn into something else. I didn't want to run the risk and bring up either of our past histories. Elaine said in relief,

"Oh good, there's a rest stop."

We pull in and it was packed with tourists, the lines to the restrooms long.

"You go first," I offered.

"Okay, I also want to look at the view tower."
I patiently wait, while my bladder struggled.

She returns and asks if I need to go, to which I

confirm and run to the line. When I get back, she's

smoking, and we get back on the freeway.

I close my eyes, trying to think of a safe
subject to bring up, until I settle on directions.

"What turn off do you take?"

"101, then Bell exit. We're almost to the 101."

It's been 20 years since I lived in Phoenix.
Many more buildings were here, and there were
more businesses along the 101.

"I can't believe how big Phoenix is now."

"Oh yes, it's big."

Traffic was bumper to bumper. It's been a

long time, driving on a freeway with all the cars

rushing by. Living in a small town like Cottonwood,

you forget the way of life in a big city.

"Here's my exit. It will take us all the way to my home. Every fast food chain is on Bell."

"This must be car dealer alley," I say as we pass many lots.
"Sure is," she replies. "Whatever car model you're looking for, it's here."

She points out various stores and restaurants she's visited and eaten at.

"How far does Bell Avenue go?" I ask, curious.

"All the way to Phoenix I think. Not sure about Scottsdale. Oh, here's my turn off." She gets off at Lake Forest Drive and says, "This is Sun City. When it was first built back in the sixties, Ruth had her home built in 1967 in a location where she and her friends could look over Sun City when they visited."

I looked at all of the homes on Lake Forest. They all looked new, like they were built yesterday.

"They sure keep it nice here," I say, "Del Webb had a nice big dream for seniors."

She opens her garage door and pulls into her

driveway.

"You have to get out before I pull in, or you can't get out."

I did as she said and looked around the neighborhood as she pulled in.

She opens the back of the PT Cruiser. It was like a movie. Everything was perfect, nice and clean. I look around and say,

"It's really nice here, nicer than I remember."

"Come on Richard, let's go in. I can take one of your suitcases."

"That's okay," I reply, "I'll take both of them. Thanks, anyway."

I was showing off. The laundry room was packed with stuff, forming a pathway.

"Let's take your stuff into the guest bedroom," Elaine said.

As I followed her, she showed me the Murphy bed and told me she would show me how it works later.

"I had a Murphy bed in Hollywood," I told her.

"Come on," she said, "let me show you the rest of the house. Here's my bedroom. I just bought that set."

"Why black chimes?" I ask.

"Just wanted something different. That's my little bathroom."

"It looks new," I remark.

"It is."

I follow her into the den and see the television.

"What size is it?"

"Sixty inches. Let me show my favorite place. It's the patio."

We went out and she sat at a nice patio table, and then lit a cigarette.

I walk out to her back yard and said, "Nice orange and grapefruit trees. They smell good."

It's good to have fresh fruit in your back yard, like Arizona. I sat down with her at the table and say,

"What do you say after twenty five years we both kind of look into space? It sure is nice out here."

"Where the heck did they come from?"

I raised my voice as two F16's flew over us.

"Oh," Elaine remarked, "those F35's fly over all day. You get used to them."

"Yeah, they're awesome. You sure they're F35's?"

"Yes, you can tell the differences in the sounds."

I silently thank the aircraft for breaking the ice.

"Do you remember the last time we saw each other? It was in Hollywood in the apartment overlooking Capital Records."

"Yes, I do. We walked Hollywood Boulevard. Can't believe that was over twenty five years ago."

We both shook our heads.

"Your aunt Ruth sure left you a very nice

place to live in Sun City in your senior years," I said.

"Yes, I really like it here. Thank you, Ruth." She says as she looks up to the heavens.

I said, "So 99th Ave is the main street off Bell to your home?"

"Yes, Bell's the main street. It goes all the way to Phoenix."

We sat, doing a lot of small talk, not knowing what to say. I didn't want to bring up the past, but why should that matter now?

"How long have you been living here? Were you here when your aunt died?"

"Oh, yes. I took care of her for five years before she passed."

"That must have been really hard," I replied.

"Yes, it was really hard, but I was there when my mother and dad passed, too, so I was kind of used to death if you can get used to a love one dying."

She had a very sad look on her face.

"You were in Minnesota?" I asked.

"Yes, I lived there for nine years and had a great time with my parents before the passed. Let's go inside. Are you getting a little hungry?"

"Yes, I could eat a bite or two."

"You watch TV while I fix us something. Are a tuna sandwich and chips okay?"

"Sounds good to me," I said.

She tunes on the 60 inch television. It was like being in a Harkins theater with the large screen. An old Western was on with Jack Palance in it. I watched one scene before I looked around. There were many things, like the new computer and some nice plants. It felt awkward being here, but we were married for 12 years and we got along when we talked on the phone for a couple of days. We used to have a great time together. She came in with two plates and handed me my half sandwich.

She said, "There are Cokes in the icebox. Help yourself."

We eat, watching the Western, not saying too much, I guess still feeling each other out after 25 years.

We watched two more old Western movies until it was almost 4:00 p.m., the two of us still not saying too much. Elaine then asked,

"What should we have for dinner? I didn't know if you could eat Mexican food every day."

"Yes, it's in my blood from my Estrada heritage," I replied, "I could eat Mexican food seven days a week."

Elaine said, "Remember all that stuff I used to make for the boys, all those food inventions?"

"Yes and the boys hated the weird concoctions," I mentioned.

"No, they liked my stuff," Elaine insisted.

"No, they didn't. They always gave a look, like, 'please, Dad, you cook'."

"Anyway, there's a little Mexican restaurant called Don Jose's. It's not too far, so we'll go there for dinner."

"We just had Mexican in Cottonwood, are you sure?"

"Yes, I love Mexican, too," she remarked. "It's time for a cigarette."

She goes out onto the patio and I follow her.

"It sure is peaceful here."

"Yes, I love it here."
We sat there small talking again. Her neighbor, Ron, poked his head around his patio and said hi. She returned the hello but didn't say anything about me.

"So," I started, "you're friends with neighbors."
"Yes, a little with Ron, but not with my roof mate anymore. We used to be friendly. I was always doing things for her, and then one day she stopped talking to me."

"That's life," I replied, "you never know. It's from one day to the next. Look at us. I never thought we'd be sitting here after all these years."

"Yes, it's something. I didn't expect it ever. I have to get a little ready."

As she got up and went in, I sat there, enjoying the moment with conflicted emotions.

The sun was going down as we drove to Don Jose's.

"It looks like all these homes were built yesterday," I remarked.

"Yes it does. Sun City has great rules about keeping your home and yard nice."

She pulled into a shopping center and parked in front of Don Jose's, which was small inside.

"I really like their food. I come here all the time."

Ten minutes later, we were already eating. The food was good, but not really Mexican food. We both chatted until our plates are empty.

"We'd better go," Elaine said, "I have to go to sleep and wake up at four-thirty."

"What, are you in the army? That's really early," I said, surprised.

"No, but on Mondays I shower and have my coffee and cigarette. I hope I don't wake you."

"Oh, no," I replied, "I wake up around that time if I am lucky; I get six hours of sleep."

"I have to get my eight hours."

She talked to the restaurant owner as I went outside. It was dark when we drove back and pulled into her driveway. I got out again before she pulled into the garage. I told her I had to use her restroom. In turn, she said she had to have her glass of wine, and that she would be waiting for me on the patio. When I finished my business, I went out and joined her as she was smoking and drinking.

"Is that the same wine you drank in Chino?"

"Yes it is. I've been drinking this wine for forty years."

"You don't get sick of the same wine?" I asked, surprised.

"No."

She lit another cigarette. I asked,

"4:30 a.m.? That early?"

"Always Mondays. As I said, I bathe, fix my hair, and put on new makeup. Will you be okay by yourself?"

"I'll be fine. Just getting out of Cottonwood will be like a vacation. It seems really nice here in Sun City. It looks like everything is in walking distance."

"Yes, everything is over there," she said as she pointed, "the Walgreens, Dollar Tree, and the Bell recreational center is several blocks that way, and McDonald's is on Bell, so there's many things to keep you busy. What time is it?"

I look at my watch and tell her the time. 8:45 p.m.

"I better go in to sleep when I finish my cigarette."

"I'm going to watch the news if that's okay," I stated.

"Sure, I'll be in and watch a little with you before I go to sleep."

A while later she comes back in and asks,

"Any good news?"

I shook my head and we watch the TV together until the weather woman appears, and Elaine says,

"I better go to sleep. Four-thirty comes fast."

As she got up, I asked her if the sound would bother her.

"No, not at all."

"See you in the morning, Elaine."

"Okay, see you too."

I played with the remote and browsed the channels. I only had 20 in Cottonwood, but there were over 200 channels included everything: sports, cooking, game shows. I was fighting to keep my eyes open, so I turned the set off and went into the guest bedroom. The Murphy bed was made up. I lay there and looked up at the ceiling, thinking about her. It seemed like old times when we were in our 20's. A warm feeling came over me. Could it really be, after all these years, I still love her? Now a senior, so many years have passed. I closed my eyes and ready to go to sleep.

I hear her in the bathroom. The clock beside me reads 5:40 a.m. I must have slept like a baby. I go into the den and sit there, which is still dark, trying to wake up, when she comes in.

"Good morning, Elaine."
She jumps a foot in the air and yelps,

"You scared me."

"Sorry about that."

"I'm used to being by myself. I'm going out for a smoke."

It was cold, so I used one of her jackets.

"Did you sleep well on the Murphy bed?" she asked.

"Like a baby. It was the best night's sleep in a long time. What about you?"

"Oh, I always sleep well."

Traffic was picking up on the street.

"How long have you been working these hours?" I asked.

"Two years. It's better than nine to five with your whole day gone. All I did was watch TV, eat, and go to sleep. I like these hours a lot better."

She's had four cigarettes in a short time.

"Well, I better get dressed."

"I'll make some coffee. I only drink decaf."

"That's what I drink," I said in kind.

She went in, while I watched the sun light up

the morning sky. The birds started singing above, and a rabbit hopped by. I felt good being out of Cottonwood. My brother, Wally, is now only 20 miles away, so I should go visit him and his lady Connie for a weekend before I go back.

When I head back in, the coffee was ready, as I predicted. I add my milk and sugar. She came from her bedroom, looking like the Elaine I used to know, all dolled up. She dressed like a million dollars.

"Nice outfit," I said.

"Thanks."

"Is there anything I can do for you?"

"No, maybe later on," she replied. "There's a list of TV channels to watch. I'm running late."

She fixes herself a peanut butter jelly sandwich. I watch her run around, doing what working people do, buzzing around like a bee in the morning.

"I have to go. See you around three."

"Okay."

I watch her drive off in her white PT Cruiser. When she left, I did the dishes. Here I was, in this nice home in Sun City. It was only seven in the morning. No stores were open, so I watch TV for a couple hours.

I head out in front of her house and look both ways. Several seniors were walking their dogs. Oh my god, this is dog heaven. I brought my business cards with me and went outside to watch the golfers drive their go-carts.

I counted 20 seniors walk by with their canine best friends. Many breeds were there, but they were mostly small dogs. I felt kind of like a new person here. I went back inside and fixed myself a bowl of cornflakes.

I sat down at the TV and browsed the channels.

This was fun, how do I make up my mind what to watch? About after twenty minutes of flipping through them, I go back to the Western channel. Mr. Peck was in this movie. It was about 9:30 p.m., so I decide to go check the shopping mall.

Some ladies were coming in as I went out and we all smiled. I like this place. A small bus was parked out in front.

"What's that about?" I asked myself.

Seniors were coming out of the visitor center.

"Good morning sir. How can I help you?" A man said.

"Good morning to you," I said in turn. "That bus out front, what's going on?"

"Oh, that's our tour bus of the Sun City Recreational Center. Would you like to take a tour next time?"

"Yes. I would get to see the entire recreational center here in Sun City?"

"You sure do."

"Sign me up for the next tour."

He did so as I checked all the little newspapers from Sun City. I took several of them so that I could read what's going on here, including the daily news and other tidbits. My hands were full of them.

My watch read 12:20 p.m. Elaine said there was a McDonald's on Bell Road. It was time for a drink and some fries.

I go to the light at 99th Ave and Bell, which just turned green. There were 32 seconds for me to cross.

There were more cars as I crossed both ways than in Cottonwood. There was a fire station on 99th Ave. I looked all around to see everything. It was like a new adventure with so many stores to check out, even an Arthur Murray dance studio. I saw the McDonald's sign to left and went in. It was full, with three lines at the counter, and no seats were empty. I waited and finally got a seat at the counter and set my hat down on it.

I went to get my drink and fries. Nearly everyone there were seniors, all having a nice lunch, telling jokes to each other. Most of them looked in good shape like they were taking good care of themselves. Some were nice looking women and men; some were reading books, while others were reading newspapers. I wish I had my

paper and writing stuff.

"How are you doing today?" I asked a man
next to me.

"Really good, I'm still talking and walking."

I agreed with him.

"Where are you from?" He asked.

"Cottonwood."

"Where?"

"It's by Sedona."

"Everyone knows Sedona," he said.

"And you?"

"Kansas City."

We continued to make small talk back and
forth while I try to eat my fries.

He left, and I refilled my drink and headed

out to a bakery and a secondhand store in the

mall. The bakery was busy, with people of all ages buying various goodies. I bought some cookies and got a senior discount. Next time I'll check out the second hand store. I have to come back to McDonald's and do some writing. I did most of my writing at fast food places during the 40 years that I've done it. It was a nice day here.

As I walked back to Elaine's place, walking a different route, I saw the same things: the new homes, and there was a new golf course behind the homes. A man was washing his old Corvette, a 1960 model, I thought. We nodded at each other. In about 20 minutes, I was back in her neighborhood, but I didn't know which home was hers. I had to take a hard look at the flag in the front yard.

It was her house, so I sat on the front porch for a little bit, watching some wild looking golf cart zoom by. I drank too much Coke, so I hurried inside. After I finished my business, I didn't feel like watching TV, so I read Florence Henderson's <u>Life is not a Stage</u>.

It was a very good read. Many bad and good things happened to Florence. I turned on the radio really low and listened to it as I read, until I heard the garage door open. I waited by the kitchen door.

"Hi," I said, "so, how was your day, or should I ask?"

I take her water bottle.

"Don't ask. It's the same thing every day, every month. I have to go to the restroom."

I watch TV, standing there, waiting for her.

She came back and fixed herself a vodka,

and then we went out in to the patio.

"You really don't like your job," I said.

"I said before I hated it. I like the people I work for: Debbie, Donna, Bill, and my little Sugar."

"Who's this Sugar?"

"Oh, a little black long haired Chihuahua.

"It's it time to shave that beard off, don't you think?" She asked. "You've had it for twenty five years and you'll look a lot better without it. That gray beard makes you look older."

"I have been thinking about cutting it off. Maybe I will. That really was something last night. I didn't think I had it in me."

She takes big gulps and is smoking.

"Yes it was something," she replied that was all that what was said.

It broke the ice. Love making always does. She

went in to fix herself another glass of vodka. My

watch says it is 4:45 p.m.

She came back out and asked, "What do you feel like eating?"

"Whatever you fix. I will eat most anything. Don't you remember I'm not a picky eater; you fix it, I will eat it?"

She laughs and says,

"I don't feel like cooking. Let's go out to eat. What about Red Lobster?"

"Sure." Beggars can't be choosers.

"Well, let's go," she said.

"Are you okay to drive after those vodkas?" I asked.

"Oh, I'm fine."

She could always hold her alcohol more than I could. We drove, and were almost at Red Lobster when she cut off a motorcyclist. He waved his fist at us.

"Didn't you see that motorcyclist?"

"No," she said.

"That was a close one."
She didn't say anything. Maybe she shouldn't

be drinking and driving at her age. I drop it. We

park there. The line was big, and it would be a 40

minute wait. We sat outside while she smoked. I

asked,

"You come here often?"

"Every two months with my working friends. I
like my shrimp and steak."
A lot of people were waiting. At least it was a

nice evening. Finally our buzzer went off. They

seated us by the bar. A nice young waitress took

our order. Elaine ordered a glass of wine, and I

ordered a Coke. It was 7:00 p.m. when we got our

dinner. We both ordered steak and shrimp.

"This is really good food," I said, "I can't
remember the last time I went to a nice restaurant."

"Well, enjoy."

It was 8:00 p.m. when we pulled into the garage, both of us stuffed.

"We have enough food for two for meals," she said.

I turn on the TV and watch an old movie. She went into her bathroom and came back, then sat in her favorite seat. I could tell she was partially drunk just after watching TV for ten minutes. She then asked,

"Can I ask you something?"

"Sure."

"Why did you leave me for some cult religion?"

"Well, to begin with, it wasn't a cult, it was the I Am religion, and I wanted to stop drinking and smoking, which I did."

"That was a cult."

"No it wasn't. That was what Jesus tried to teach mankind. I Am that I Am and we are the likeness of God."

"No, that's a cult."

We went back and forth for 20 minutes. The alcohol was talking.

"I'm going to bed," I got up, leaving her. I didn't need to bring up the past again. That was long ago. Here we are today, making love, having a good time together. Why bring up the past?

I lay there, my head upset. I thought after all these years, she had changed. How can she be drinking all these years? I finally went to sleep. I woke up around 6:00 a.m. and went out the bedroom. She was still knocked out on the sofa. I finished my business in the restroom, and then went to take her up.

"Elaine, are you going to work? It's 20 after 6."

"Oh no, I'm running late."

She jumps up and hurries into the bathroom.

I fix some coffee, and then ask her, "Do you want a cup?"

"Yes," she yells back.

She runs around, hurriedly preparing. I watch the news. She went out to smoke. I didn't feel like talking, because the possibility of last night may come up.

"See you after work," she says.

I did some house work: cleaned out her laundry room, which held two cases of wine and a big bottle of vodka; dusted inside the living room, and other tasks. I did all of my house cleaning back in Cottonwood.

I had to get out, just go for a walk around the neighborhood. I checked out the golf course. Many people were playing. I watched as I walked. I tried golf once, and I could hit the ball straight. Ladies and men were walking by with various breeds and sizes of dogs.

I walked by two churches on the way to Bell Street. A family taco shop was on the other side of the street. I headed down Bell to get back to 99th Ave back to Elaine's. I thought about last night. I guess she wants to know why I left in 1980. I guess she had the right hope that was it for the last night?

I stopped by a post office on the way. My legs were getting tired, so I went in and had some pie and coffee. While there, I looked at an Arizona Republic newspaper while I rested my old legs. 25 minutes later, the seniors coming in for a late lunch were arriving, so I went back out on my trek to 99<sup>th</sup> Ave. I thought perhaps I took too long of a walk. There were a lot of stores and stops, and finally there was 99<sup>th</sup> Ave. I could see the McDonald's. Maybe I could go there tomorrow and do some writing. I cross the street and go see the Bell recreational center. I watch men play pool and rest. This really is a city built for seniors. I continue to watch them for half an hour.

Better get going. It was like being in a brand new world. I go back outside to my path. Along the way, there's a senior woman who was washing her car. It had a "For Sale" sign on the window. I greeted her, "Hi. Nice day. You're selling your new car and it's only a year old?"

"Yes, I need to sell my new car to give

money to my niece for college. Her parents and my son are having hard times, and I want to help them."

"Yes, there are many parents having a hard time these days."

"Are you interested? It's a very good deal. $9,000 today."

"I am looking for a good used car, but that's out of my budget. Thanks, and have a nice day."

I walk off and wait for the light to turn green at the intersection. I like reading the sign that counted off the seconds.

Three days have passed. She comes home from work and drinks wine. It wasn't so bad when she drinks wine, but that vodka makes a big difference. Saturday morning, and we are out on the patio, having our coffee. She drinks and smokes.

"I feel like doing something today after my show," she said, "I have to see my man Cheyenne."

I just roll my eyes and shake my head a little. A big crow lands by a bush. She gets up and runs it off.

"I hate those crows. They eat my baby quail."

She lights another cigarette and says,

"I haven't been to the Scottsdale farmers market in a long time. Let's go there and have breakfast. I like their omelets. They're really big and good. You'll like them. Sound good to you?"

"Yes, doing whatever you feel like is good. Just getting out of Cottonwood is good."
So we watch Cheyenne on the TV. There's

no talking. She becomes part of the show. She

loves her Westerns. We get dressed and go on our

way to some place in Scottsdale. It's not too busy

for a Saturday morning. I ask her,

"When was the last time you were at this market?"

She's smoking with the window open, thank God.

"Maybe a year ago. When I came here, it was a small market with lots of artists trying to sell their art."

We pull into a long, small driveway. The parking was limited, so we had to wait for a car to pull out. It was a two minute wait.

"We lucked out."

Many cars were waiting for parking. We got out and watched a couple come out, their arms full of stuff.

"They look happy," Elaine said.

Both sides were lined with artists, displaying their works of art to everyone with big smiles, hoping you'll stop and buy their pieces. We look around. Elaine stops to look at some nice jewelry. I look at everything, wishing I had brought my video camera. At least I had my cards to give out at the busy farmers market, which was a normal driveway during the weekdays.

"What do you think of this piece of jewelry?" Elaine asked.

"Very nice."

She puts it up to her neck.

"Think I should buy it?"
"It's nice. That's up to you."

"No, I have to look around some more."

The artist looked disappointed.

The food vendors were selling their stuff and giving out free samples, some of which we ate. Elaine said, after taking one,

"I really like this bread, but we have to have their famous omelets. You can add anything in it: cheese; bacon; they have it, and it's so big you can't eat the whole thing."

"I can smell it."

I lick my lips kidding. There's a whole bank of

cooking tables, with workers behind them making

omelets for a line of people, all of them licking their

lips.

"We have to find a table first," she said. "What do you want on your omelets? You wait for a table, and I'll order."

All the tables were filled with families and

couples enjoying themselves, while a small jazz

band was playing.

It was a nice day in Scottsdale just watching

everyone. It was a treat. Some people had dogs

with them. I have to give my cards to the dog

lovers.

Several folks were waiting for tables, but I

was there first. I finally found an open table right

across from the jazz band. Elaine was in line, and

it wasn't long until she came over with her arms

full.

"Here's your surprise. It has a little of everything, like mine. Don't eat yet, I have to get our champagne and OJ."

The smell of eggs mixed with bell peppers, bacon, and several other ingredients made my mouth water. She came back with two small glasses. We eat and listen to the jazz, enjoying ourselves.

"Isn't this fun and taste good?" She asked.

"Yes, thanks a lot."

A group next to us had an older hound dog with begging eyes, so we both feed him.

"Well, here go our leftovers for tonight," Elaine said.

We couldn't resist his sad eyes. His owner were busy, eating and laughing a lot to each other's jokes. After breakfast, we look around some more. I have out ten cards to people with

dogs. She didn't buy anything.

"Let's go see Wally," I brought up. "They can't be too far from here. I'll give him a call that we are coming over for a visit."

"When was the last time you saw your brother Wally?"

"I can't remember. That's how long it's been."

"Now, he's with a lady named Connie, you said."

"Yes, she's a very nice woman after his long bad marriage."

I call him and tell her,

"He wants us to have lunch with him. I couldn't say no."

"I don't think I can eat anything," she replied, "I'm too stuffed."

"Maybe we'll eat just a bit," I suggested.

She raised her eyebrows as if to say "no."

In about ten minutes we pull into their driveway.

"I'm so stuffed," we both say and laughed.

Their three dogs were barking at the gate. Wally came out and stopped the hounds.

"Hey bro," I said, "Remember Elaine?"

Connie's there too. We all hug. I patted Wally's old female dog and asked her,

"Puka, do you remember me?"

Elaine and Connie were chatting.

Wally said, "Just in time for lunch. Hope you guys are hungry. Want to check out this place?"

I took the tour, while Elaine and Connie went inside.

"This place is big and nice," I said.

There was an above ground pool that looked inviting during the hot summer time. My brother said,

"Let's go in and have lunch."

I follow him inside. Connie had a big spread

of sandwich fixings. Elaine fixed us both half a sandwich. Nickie, their niece, arrives.

"Meet Nickie."

"Hi, Nickie," we both said.

We look at each other and try to eat. Connie shows us the inside of the home.
"You have a very nice home, Connie," Elaine said.

We sat and watched TV using their 70 inch TV. We stayed for two hours, making small talk. Elaine was giving me the eye, indicating it was time to go. We said our farewells and hugged each one another.

We were back in Sun City in about twenty minutes and back to her home. It was 3:30 in the afternoon. I went to the restroom, and when I came out, Elaine was fixing herself a vodka with 7-Up. I made a face to myself. I guess she has to have her alcohol.

"That was a nice visit," I said, "how did you like Connie?"

"I like her a lot," she replied. "It's too bad she has all those health problems. Wally looks pretty good for working under the hot Arizona sun all his life."
"Yes, I don't know how he's able to lay out brick in the 110 degree weather."

"And I didn't see anything wrong with Nickie. You said she had seizures."

We went out on to the patio so she could smoke and continued to make conversation. I accidentally let it slip out,

"Do you have to drink every day?"

Anger contorted her face.

"Don't bug me about my drinking. This is what I like to do every weekend."

She finishes her drink and goes inside to prepare another one. I walk around the yard and try to see over the wall. There's a police car on the other side.

"What's going on?" I ask aloud.
"I don't know," she said back. "I need to be six inches taller to see over this wall."

She lights up another cigarette and tries to keep the smoke away from me. It works for about half of the time. Out of nowhere she brings up,

"I bought that dark beer for you. Why haven't you had one?"

"I only have a beer three or four times a year. Maybe I will drink one."

I got up and fetched one.

"It's been years since I've had a dark beer."

"It's too bad we gave that dog all our leftovers. We could have had them for dinner," Elaine remarks.

She finishes her second vodka and goes

back inside for another drink. This time, she came

out with a big glass of wine. I could tell she was

getting very drunk. I had to watch what I say so I

don't set her off. She tells me,

"What happened to you? You look bad. You used to dress sharply, and that beard looks terrible. You really should shave it off. I'll do it for you."

Here we go. I listened to her for about 25 minutes, talking about how badly I looked. I drink half of my beer, listening to how much I changed. Why did I dress like a bum? I didn't think that I looked bad.

This happened over the next three days. She would get on me about something. I was getting to the point that I didn't want to be here anymore, but with no car, what could I do?

She was like a different person when she didn't drink. That damn vodka. We had a good time, otherwise, together; I was torn between what to do.

Do I go or stay? Maybe I should say something. I tried, but she doesn't think she has a problem, and that will most likely start a big fight.

We made love back in those days. It was good to see we still love each other. Last night, we both said "I love you" at the same time. We held each other until we went to sleep. The next morning, she is in her bathroom. I fix some coffee and go out on to the patio. I was conflicted about what to do, my thoughts and feelings going in all sorts of directions. Here I am, back again with the one woman I only ever truly loved. That deep love was back, and I felt like a teenager. Everything looked great, and as they say, love never dies. Maybe I can overlook her drinking, or get used to it.

I never thought I would be in love again.

When I feel this love overcome me, since it had

never actually left me, everything, the colors of the

world, looks more vibrant. I can't get over it.

The coffee must be ready, so I go back in and ask her,

"Want a cup?"

"Yes."

She comes out of the restroom and we greet each other with our
"Mornings" and a little kiss, as if we had never been apart.

"So, what's the plan for today?" I ask her as I pour her coffee and add cream."

"Have you been to West World?"

"No. Is that a part of Sun City?"

"No, no. It's a big entertainment center next to the Cardinal stadium. It has every restaurant you can think of. It's really great there. It gets so busy after games, you can't move."

"That sounds fun. Yes, I'd like to see this West World."

We drank our coffee and ate our toast.

"We'll have a late brunch," she said.

"That will be a nice surprise, and I have a surprise for you," I replied.

"What is it? I like surprises. What is it? Can't you say?"

"I will show you this evening."

"Okay, okay."

We went inside and got dressed. Twenty minutes later we were pulling into West World. There was a big hotel on the left. Parking was easy.

"This is really big," I said to myself.

All kinds of cars were here already. There were people with kids, and many lovers holding hands. I asked her,

"Do you come here often?"

"Oh, just once in a while with my coworkers."

"No Cardinals game?" I asked her.

"No, not yet. Maybe we can go to a game this year."

"Yeah, that would be fun."

We held hands and walked around the mall.

We sat watching everyone

"I bet this mall looks a lot different night all those lights lit, with all of this night life we would be lucky to get a seat," I said.

"Oh yes it's the show place, we'll have to come here for dinner one night," Elaine said.

We both sat for another 10 minutes.

"I'd like to check out the hotel next door," I said.

So we walked on over.

As we were walking over I noticed another

big mall across the street Elaine said she would

take me there next time we were in town.

We looked over and saw a large limo pulling up in front of the hotel.

Elaine thought out loud, "maybe it's a movie star."

However, when the driver opened the door three businessmen in suits got out. We decided to follow them into the big hotel. It's been a long time since I've been in a first class hotel. The Verde Valley doesn't even have a mall.

I was like a kid in candy store checking everything out. I looked at the bar, all over the lobby, and it even had a nice water fall. To Elaine this must be old hat because she's from around the city. For me it was fun, the last big cities I had seen were Hollywood and LA. That was 25 years ago.

"Have you seen enough? I am getting hungry for Mexican Food," said Elaine

I said, "Sounds good to me."

"I feel like a baby again everything's new to me. I haven't been in the city and a longtime."

We're back on the 101 freeway.

I just look at everything trying to learn where things are in case I have to drive here again.

Several more stoplights and she pulls into a parking lot at a Mexican restaurant.

"Good time for lunch," I said.

We when into the place, it was only half full.

"It smells good in here."

I being half white and half Mexican love my Mexican Food. I order a giant burro, Mexican rice, beans, flour tortillas, and a coke.

She orders the three been taco and a mix drink.

"Let's go outside and eat," she said.

I followed her. We had the whole patio to ourselves.

"Boy, doesn't this taste good," she remarked.

I agreed with my mouth full
We were too busy eating to talk; just enjoying the moment.

"So what is this big surprise you've been waiting to show me?" she asked.

I replied, "You'll see and you will be really surprised."
Her eyes look all excited as she took a big drink. More people came out on the patio as we finished eating.

She lit up a cigarette as we walked to the car. I just stand there while she smokes.

"No, you wouldn't guess it in a million years," I commented.

"Now I'm really excited," she said.
.

We were back at her place I when into the kitchen door and poured myself a glass of water, Elaine stayed on the back porch smoking her cigarette.

As I came back out on the patio she noticed I had my right hand closed in a fist.

"What are you doing?" she said.

"Is this the surprise?" she asked excitedly.
I open my right hand slowly; her eyes almost pop down.

In my hands were wedding bands, I kept them all these years.  She was stunned.

"Those are our wedding rings from when we first got married in Phoenix, you kept them all these years?"

"Have you tried them on in all those years?" She asked.

"No."

"Let's try them on now."

"I can't believe they still fit after all these years.  Was this meant to bring us back together?"

"Only God knows, here we are after all these years."

Up we show each other our fitting rings.
"I still can't believe you saved them.  I have to call all my girlfriends and tell them," Elaine said.

As she is getting up, I exclaim "Now!?"

"Yes", she said excitedly "They're not going to believe me."
We kiss.

"Love you," I whispered.

"I love you, too."

She goes into the living room and makes her calls. I wait a minute and then follow her into the room

There, she is excitedly telling the story to her friend Donny.

"You won't believe what Richard did; he just showed me our wedding rings from home we got married 35 years ago here in Phoenix"

I went back outside.

She called three other ladies.

She was on the phone for an hour.

As I sat watching the birds she came out side with me carrying a glass of one.

"What did your lady friends say about our

rings?" I asked.

"None of them could believe you saved them all of these years."
"That was real romantic," she said softly.

"It's kind of like you keeping your last name Corey maybe this is meant to bring us back together after all these years, the past is the past what happens now is all that matters."

"You're right the past is the past, now that we're seniors we will have each other."

She gently played with the ring on her finger.

"It still fits like it was yesterday."

"I need a nap."
"Me, too."

We lay down on the bed together arms

wrapped around each other each of us saying we

love the other.  She went to sleep.  I just laid there

for a moment wondering what was happening

here.  I had that deep feeling of love for her.  It was

all coming back. That loving feeling, and it felt great. But it was all happening so fast, especially at our age. As they say love never dies. Her drinking came to mind. Maybe I can live with it. I soon fell asleep.

Two days pass. We were talking about us getting married again and me moving in with her. That would mean me moving out of Cottonwood, selling all my things, setting up new doctors. It would be quite a change from Cottonwood, a small city, a slow life, to Phoenix, a big city with lots of life. All of these changes were going through my head. It's time for her to come from work. I was hoping she would have a glass of wine not that terrible vodka. She was like night and day. When she came in, I helped her with her packages as always do.

"Should I ask how your day was?"
We kissed; she gave me a small smile.

"Don't ask. I need a drink."

I sat in the den as she poured herself something to drink.

When she came in the room I saw it was a glass of wine. I was relieved.

"Come on, patio time," she said.

We sat on the patio for a while her smoking and drinking. That was part of her life a regular routine.

It was Wednesday morning about 6:30 a.m.

Elaine was in the kitchen fixing her lunch, getting

ready for work.

"Morning," she said

"Yes, morning. I woke up at five with this nagging headache."

I sat in the den holding my head.

"Did you take some aspirin?"

"No, not yet."

"Here I'll get you some."

"Thanks."

I took the aspirin followed by the big glass of water.

"I'm going back to bed I hope those aspirin work, I don't feel good."

"Okay, I hope they work, I will call you from work."

"Love you."

"Love you, too."

I lay in the guest room with my eyes closed trying to sleep. I heard her drive off to work. I had set the phone on the floor next to the bed so it'd be easy to get two when she called. My watch was next to me. I tried to sleep but headache would not go way.  The phone rang it was 9:00 a.m.

"Hi, how are you feeling", she asked.

"Oh, it feels like it's getting a little better, I lie"

"Oh good, can't talk long.  It's the first of the month and I am very busy.  I will call again bye."

My headache was getting real bad.  I was trying to get up to go to the restroom.  When I sat up I was dizzy.  I couldn't stand up so I try to crawl on my hands and knees to the restroom.  I only made it to the bedroom door.  I crawled back to the bed.  I was seeing everything double.  What the hell was going on now?  I could see two fans above me standing, and I knew there was only one.  I was very dizzy and have double vision.  I close my eyes it seemed Okay.  Every time I raise my head I got real dizzy.  I tried to get up again, but couldn't.  I didn't want to fall over and hurt

myself.  I put one leg over the side of the bid to see

if it would help.  It didn't, so I just laid there with my

eyes closed.

I woke up to the phone ringing.

"Hi, how' you doing is your headache getting any better"

"A little, I think it will be okay", I lie again as most men do about their health.

"Do you want me to come home?"

"No, no I'll be okay."

"Okay, I have to finish this end of the month book work, I'll try to come home early, love you."

"Me, too."

I didn't want to take her away from her work.

I have had migraines in the past.  But this was

worse.  The last time I was in Hollywood that one

put me in the hospital.  It was a cluster migraine.  I tried to raise my head on my elbow.  Then my head started pounding like it was going to explode.

I had a special pill for migraines I had gotten over 25 years ago.  They were old but in Cottonwood, lots of good that did me here.  If only I had brought some aspirin and water with me this morning I lay down.  This migraine is different.

"Dear Lord help me," I said to myself.

I couldn't do anything except lay there.  I looked at my watch and it was 2:00 p.m.  She should be coming home soon.  She I can go to the store and purchase some over the counter migraine pills.  I open my eyes and still have double vision. I raise up my arm over my head.  It helps for some reason.  In a dark room, I lay back down.  The pounding inside my head was 10 times worse.  Like that week back in Hollywood.  I heard the bedroom door open.

"How are you doing," Elaine asked.

"I am real sick."

She felt my head.

"Your hot, come on am taking you to the hospital, get up."

"I can't, I feel very dizzy and have double vision, and I think I might fall."

"What?  That doesn't sound like a bad headache."

"You have to help me to the car."

I stood up she put my arm around her shoulder.  I tried to take a step we both almost fell. I couldn't walk I was real dizzy.  We both kind of lay back on the bed. "I don't know what is wrong with me."

"Come on we have to get you to the hospital now".  Use the walls and lean on me," she said

We made by using the walls, the dresser top, door jams, and the kitchen counter. Each step was difficult. We almost fell over several times. I just couldn't balance myself.

"I don't know if I can make it," I said.

"Yes you can. Only a little further the go."

"I'll have to put you in the backseat."

She was having a hard time holding me up and opening the doors.

"Lean on the door."

We are in the car going down Lake Forest Drive. I closed my eyes. The bright sun was making my head pound harder, it seemed. I can't believe we are hitting every damn red light.

"How are you doing?" she asked.

"My head my head "I really felt like my head

was going to explode.  It seemed like forever before we got to the hospital.

"Here we are, just wait there.  I'll get a nurse and wheel chair."

They open the car door.  I almost fell out. Both of them had to catch me and help me into the wheel chair.

"How are you doing, sir."

"Let's get you into the emergency room, now."

The nurse was asking Elaine questions about me.  No waiting in the lobby.  I was rushed to a small emerge see room immediately.  They put me in a big chair.  One nurse was asking you Elaine questions one was taking my blood pressure.

"Oh my god," I heard a nurse say

"196/205, call for a bed now."

"Can you do something for my head? It feels like it's going to explode now," I said.

Elaine could see the pain in my face; I could see the worry look on hers face.

"They're trying to get you a room now. There just aren't any available."

Elaine was holding my hand.

The nurse took my blood pressure again.

"My head, my head!"

"Can't you give him something for his head?" Elaine asked nurse Reedley.

The nurse said no we would have to wait for

the doctor. It shouldn't be to long before we have a

room ready. She shook her head worried about

the blood pressure. After several minutes they

rushed me into hospital ward. The orderly was just

finishing the bed. I guess it was real busy here.

They helped me into bed. I did know how long I

could take my head pounding before something

really bad happened.  I was holding my head with both hands as if that would help.  My head my head give me something for my head.  Just then a doctor came in.  She talked to Elaine.

"Mr. Corey, I am Dr. Ruth.  I'm going to help you now.  What seems to hurt you?"

"He says his head is about to explode, can you please give him something now?!" Elaine almost shouted.

The doctor ordered several nurses to do this and that put needles in both arms one was still taking blood pressure she whispered something to Elaine.  "It's a good thing you brought in now or it may have been too late.  His blood pressure is really high."  They began giving me the morphine and saline the doctor talking to nurses.

"Is it helping yet? The morphine shouldn't take long to work," said Dr. Ruth.

I tried to look at Elaine now. I felt bad for her having to bring me to the hospital.

"Richard, can you open your eyes?"

I did.

"The morphine should be working soon, you feel it."

"Yes," shaking my head a little, "What's wrong with me?"

"They're sure you're having a stroke, but they don't know what kind of stroke. They are going to have to do a lot of tests to determine that." Elaine said

My head was getting little better by the minute.

"A stroke? One day I am okay and the next day a stroke?"

"Yes, that's what they say," said Elaine

"How can I be okay one day the next day in the hospital with a stroke? No, I think it's just a bad migraine like in Hollywood."

"Well, we'll have to see what the doctors find when they start testing."

Another doctor comes into the room, a male, looks like he's from another country. The doctor introduced himself he said his name but it was so long I didn't catch it.  He said he was going to have me do some exercises in hour.  He would be checking all my vital signs, then said something to Elaine and left.

"I'm sorry about this.  I don't even remember changing into this hospital dress.  I thought my head was going to explode.  What were the doctors saying?"

"They don't know anything.  You've only been here for 45 minutes.  Is the morphine working?"

"It seems to be, but my head is still hurting. The pounding is going away.  I hope there's nothing wrong with my brain.  Thank God I didn't lose it.  I feel like going to sleep."

"No, you can't, the doctor said to keep you wake for a couple of hours. They need to do several tests on you."

"What about eating something"? You haven't had any food today.
"No."

I close my eyes, two nurses and Elaine yell at me, "You can't go to sleep!"

I told them I was just resting, my eyes hurt from that pounding in my head.

I ask for some water. They would only allow me to have some ice.

"Elaine you must be must be tired from work and I feel bad this happen," I said

Elaine softly said, "Don't be silly, I will be okay"

I was almost 5:00 p.m. I knew she had to go

home and get some rest before she goes to work

tomorrow. She wanted to stay around until the

doctors at some answers and tests me. Just then a

doctor came in.

"We have a MRI room waiting for you Mr. Corey" a young male orderly said.

The orderly helped me on to a rolling bed then covered me with a new blanket.

"See you Elaine"

A doctor stayed with her saying the usual things, this won't take too long.

As he rolled me I was looking at the ceiling into the elevator down one floor out into hall way passing doctors and nurses into a lab room.

"Are you okay?" asked the orderly.

"Have you ever been in an MRI machine before?" he continued.

"I have. Don't like them, but I'm okay," I said, as the orderly help me into the machine.

"Okay, just be as still as a dead person" he said jokingly.

I simply made a face I did not find it funny.

In 10 minutes I was rolling back to my room.

Elaine wasn't there she probably went to get something to eat or have a smoke. My headache was almost gone. I felt weak and run down. Maybe I can sleep now. The nurses help me back on my bed. I close my eyes but the nurses quickly remind me not to go to sleep. They let me know the doctor will be right in.

My stomach makes this loud growling noise.

"Sounds like someone's hungry."

"Yes, I haven't eaten anything today."

"It's almost dinner time."

A new doctor walked in.

"Mr. Corey I am Dr. Jones. How are you feeling? Is your head better?"

"Yes, it's a lot better. Still have a little headache."

"I'm here to check your reflexes. I want you

to push down on my hand with your right foot."

I did as I was instructed.

"A little harder this time."

"Now your left foot."

"Harder! Harder! Is that as hard as you can push?"

"Yes."

"Your left leg is weaker. "

"Now let's try your arms."

I push down with all my might, not much there.

"Your right side seems be Okay, but your left side has been affected.  I think we have to do more testing in the next couple of days."

A tray of food was being rolled into my room.

"Looks like dinner time I'll be back."

"Oh good, food," I said happily.

The orderly said, "You have to eat what

everybody else is eating today, tomorrow I will take your order."

"I don't care what I eat just as long as its food."

Just then Elaine walked in.

"Oh good you're eating something.  Are you feeling better?  Did they find anything?  What did the doctor say?"

She gives me a little kiss.

"It looks like you're eating good hospital food; fish, rice, mixed vegetables, cake, and milk a good meal."

"Do you want some?"

"No, I had a McDonald's fish sandwich and fries.  How's your head?"

"I feel a lot better. Maybe I can go home with you."

"Oh I am sure they wouldn't let you go."

"I'm feeling a lot better, are you sure you don't want my cake?"

"No, eat everything."

Elaine watched a new nurse. "Have any doctors been in?"

"Oh good, Mr. Corey you're finished eating, I need some blood."

The nurse did her thing and then asked if I needed anything. I told her no.

I told Elaine she'd better call Wally, Annie, and Debbie and let them know what happen to me.

"You didn't answer me, have the doctors been in to see you?"

"Yes, this doctor was here checking my legs and arms to see how good they work. I think I did okay. He did say my right side was better than my left side. I know that I'm right handed."

"He was checking to find out if your right or left side was affected by the stroke. You remember, I worked in the hospital business for 30 years."

"Oh yes, you did."

The man in the next bed was getting visitors.

It sounded like two ladies, although I couldn't see anything because there was a curtain between us.

"You must be getting tired; it has been a long day for you getting up at 4:30 a.m.  Now dealing with this and me"

"Yes, I have to go pretty soon.  I have a little home work to do."

"I can't believe I'm laying here in this hospital. What's the name of this hospital?"

"Banner, and it's the best hospital in Arizona, maybe the United States."
"Oh, that's good to know."

"I better go now my legs and eyes are getting tired.  I'll call you later it's going to be hard telling them what's happened to you."

She gives me a little kiss.

"See you tomorrow after work, love you."

"Love you, too."

I closed my eyes. I was drained.  I felt my headache returning.  Please God take it away.

"Mr. Corey, I have to take you for other test," an older orderly said.

I open my eyes and just like that my headache disappeared. "Thanks, God," I said to myself.

I was taken down the hallway for more MRI

and then returned to my bed. I needed some

sleep. I lay there thinking about God and why this

happened to me. What was going to happen?

Would I have any bad effects? I didn't want to say

the word stroke. I felt it would stop my active life,

my walking my 5 miles a day. Was it over finally?

I could hear and feel nurses is coming in and

checking on me all night. I went into a deep

dream. I couldn't move my legs. No, No! That's

what happened to me when I was a kid. Please!

Please! Not again. There was my mother with her

beautiful black hair and smile just standing there.

Then a noise woke me.  An orderly was cleaning.

It must be morning.

"What a dream," I said
I push the pager button.  I needed to go to

the restroom.  I didn't want to take the chance by

myself.  I felt real weak.  Yesterday was a big drain

on my body.  I was a little shaky.  A lady nurse

came in.

"Morning, Mr. Corey. What can I do for you?"

"I just want to go to the restroom.  I'm feeling
a little shaky."

She helped me over the bathroom.  I did my

things I needed to do.  She was waiting to help me

back in bed.

"When's breakfast?"

"In about 45 minutes and I need some blood.
I'll be back."

The sun was barely coming up. It was nice to have a window. I guess I'm lucky to be looking out the window. Having a stroke could have ended my life or worse. There are all sorts of physical issues that could have occurred with a stroke. I just shook my head. "Thank you God", I softly whispered.

Nurse came back in and took more blood.

"Have you heard what kind of stroke I had?"

"No, that would be up to the doctor to tell you."

She left with my blood. I lay there knowing I wasn't out of hot water yet. I've read about strokes and their side effects. All sorts of things can go wrong or I could even have another stroke. I shook my head no.

About that time my breakfast came in.  It was a good thing; the distraction helped me change my thinking.

"Morning, are you hungry?  I have some good food for you."

She was a cute teenager with a pretty smile.

"Thanks, your smile has made my day."

She turned a little red.  She left me with a big breakfast.  Eggs, toast, ham, milk, half a grapefruit and I eat every bit.  My stomach couldn't get enough food.  The man next to me was waking up.  Strange, you're in the hospital maybe your dying or he's dying, but you've never seen each other.  I wonder if we would like each other.  There are a lot of strange things in the world.  I lay there my eyes closed.  Why did that have to happen yesterday?

What was the future with Elaine and me?

Just seeing each other after all those years and falling back in love has been wonderful, but now I feel lost. I have to stop all this thinking. All the things you hear about strokes. People I know that had bad ones, one side their body paralyzed. My left side started twitching. "Stop that! Stop that!" I said to myself. I look over myself. Arms look okay. Legs look okay. Thank God I'm okay. I turn on the TV to stop my thinking. I watch 3TV News. The wall clock says 7:30 a.m.

"Morning, Mr. Corey."

The same older man came in with a wheelchair.

"More tests today. Was breakfast good?"

"Yes, it was."

Down the halls pass rooms with more sick people and into the elevator.

I was hooked up to the EKG again, and then later that morning I was back in that tunnel for another MRI.

After the tests, I was taken back to the room. An orderly came and asked me what kind of foods I liked. I told him what I liked. My brother walked in.

"Richard, bro."

"Hey, Wally. How are you doing?"

"I'm fine. How are you doing?  What happened?"

"I don't really know.  One day I am fine, and then I'm in the hospital.  Some kind of stroke."

"What did the doctor tell you?"

"They are still doing tests on me. Did two this morning, an EKG and MRI.  They'll check them over and I will know something.  I feel pretty good though.  I thought I was having one of my migraine headaches like from the past in Hollywood.  It was bad, so Elaine brought me here.  She said I looked bad.  I couldn't even walk.

"Connie and Nickie send their love and are saying a prayer for you"

"Good, thank them."

"Is there anything I can do for you?"

"You're doing it by being here."
We visited for a couple of hours.  We both

had our ups and downs in life.  He finally found a

good lady in Connie.  I was hoping me and Elaine

would be together in our senior years, even if she

did have a drinking problem.  My lunch was being

rolled in.

"I'm going to take off, you sure I can't get you something?"

"No, I am fine. You want some of my lunch?"

"No, you need it."

"Love you, Wally."

"Love you too, bro."

I was just finishing my lunch as my phone started to ring.

"Hello."

"Oh, hi sis."

Her voice was all shaky. You could tell she was crying. It was my sister Anna. i called her Annie.

"I'm so sorry for what happened to you. How are you doing? What have they said about your stroke?"

"I'm doing okay. They are still doing tests on me. They're not sure what I had. I don't think I had a stroke."

"Oh, Elaine thinks you did."

"Well the doctors have to check all the tests first. I seem okay. If you were here I would look the same. No side effects. Thank God"

"Yes thank God, what happened?"

"Yesterday, I was so dizzy and was having double vision.  I couldn't walk my head felt like it was going to explode.  Thank God I was at Elaine's.  I don't know what would have happen if I was home by myself in Cottonwood.  Maybe I would have died."

"Don't say that. Thank God you were at Elaine's!  And she had the sense to rush you to the hospital.  She called last night, but I waited till today to call knowing you needed your rest.  Oh, Lance, Lloyd, and Craig send their love and get better soon we're all praying for you."

"Thank them."

"Are you sure you're okay?"

"Yes, it's all in God's hands now.  I feel pretty good."

"Cheyenne sends a licking kiss."

"And I send the old lady dog Cheyenne a licking kiss back."

We both laugh

"Love you brother."

"Love you too sister."

Just then a nurse came in.
"I need more blood, Mr. Corey."

"Sis, the nurse just came in and a doctor's with her."

"Okay, I'll call you back later. Love you Richard."

"Love you too, Annie."

"Mr. Corey how are you feeling today?" asked the doctor. This was the same doctor with a big long name I couldn't say or read.

I felt pretty good after going through that terrible yesterday.

"Is your headache completely gone?"

"Almost, just a trace of it. Did you check my EKG and MRI?"

"I and several other doctors are checking both of them now. But we need to do one more MRI later today."

The doctor checked my heart and pulse

"You look surprisingly good considering what

you looked like when you first came in yesterday."

"What kind of stroke do you think I had?"

"I can't say until we check all the tests. Another doctor will be in shortly to check your reflexes."
They always did that. They will be checking them several times. The doctor said he would be back later. He left. I felt tired. Maybe I can take a little nap. The wall clock read 2:00 p.m. Elaine will be here soon. I turned off the TV but could hear my neighbors just as good. When I closed my eyes I started thinking. What was next with me? Will be the same as before? Will I be able to keep busy in my senior years or have to stop all of the things I'm used to doing? Will it be a whole different life? Someone touched my arm, I opened my eyes, and it was Elaine with her pretty face and

a little smile.

"How you feeling?"

"A lot better than yesterday.  I still don't know what happened to me."

"I was really scared."  "You couldn't even walk.  Your blood pressure was so high.  They didn't know if you're going to make it."

Tears came to her eyes.  I squeeze her hand.

"God didn't want me, yet. I feel pretty good today."

"Are you sure everything is okay?"

"Look at me, do I look the same?"

"Yes, but it's only been one day.  They need to check all your tests to find out if there's any damage from the stroke."

"I'll don't think I had a stroke."

"The doctors and nurses said you did have some kind of a stroke, the test will say what kind."

The new doctor came in to check my

reflexes.

"Hi, you two, wanted to see how you doing today."

He tested my legs first I pushed as hard as I could.

"That's real good Mr. Corey, now your hands."

I gave it everything I had; I wanted to look good in front of Elaine.

"That's good, but your left side is still a little weak. I don't think you'll be here much longer. You look much better than yesterday. What a difference a day makes. Hope things work out for both of you."

As the doctor left, Elaine asked, "Why did he say that? Did you talk to him yesterday? What did the doctor say to you yesterday?"

"They just said that with high blood pressure you're lucky if you didn't have brain damage"

Tears came to Elaine's eyes again.

"No, no, you can see that I'm okay."

"I'm going to go outside and have cigarette"

She just needed to go and get some fresh

air.  It had to be real hard seeing me after all those

years.  We fall back in love and now this happens.

Now, tears came to my eyes.  Why did this have to

happen now?  She came back with a cup of coffee.

"What day is it? I lost track of time."

"Today? Thursday and I have to get going.  I
have to pick up work mail.  All the ladies at work
are saying a prayer for you."

"Thank them all for me."

We kiss a little kiss.

"See you tomorrow, love you."

"Love you, too."

It's now Friday.  I have to have more tests

and more blood drawn.  I felt myself getting

stronger.  A little light headed it's probably all that

blood there taking and all the tests. I actually felt like I could go home. Well at least to Elaine's house. I'll ask the Doctor today. Breakfast came in. It's what I ordered: Oatmeal and wheat toast. I turned on the TV and that's pretty much what I did for the rest of the morning. I looked at the clock and it was 11:30 a.m. It was time for lunch.

"Mr. Corey, how are you doing today?"

The same lady Doctor I saw on the first day, I think. I've seen so many doctors. I couldn't remember any of their names. They were all great and   always ready to help you.

"I feel good; I think I could go home today."

She made a funny face. The kind of a face that you see when someone says, "You are kidding right?"

"I don't think you are there yet. Maybe after

physical therapy.  We'll see how you are doing then."

"What is this physical therapy?"

"As soon as there is an empty bed, you're going over to our therapy hospital.  We want to put you through some tests and see how you're doing. If you pass all the tests then you can go home.  But that could take days."

"What do you mean days?"

"Well it usually takes a couple of weeks to get your strength back.  Everyone is different. There should be a bed opening Saturday.  I do have to say you look surprisingly good for going through a stroke."

"Oh, have all you doctors checked the test to see what happened to me."

"We are still checking.  We all have to get together first.  Here comes your lunch.  See you later today."

"Thank you, doctor."

"Are you hungry?" a lady orderly said.

"I'm always ready to eat.  I like your hospital

food.  Who said hospital food was bad?"

She smiled.

"I like the food here, too.  We have good cooks here at Banner."

"Do you know anything about the Banner physical therapy facilities?"

"No, I'm just an orderly.  You have to ask the nurses and doctors.  Enjoy your lunch."

I watch television.  My neighbor was having more visitors.  He must live around here.  He seems to have lots of family.  I'm just waiting for my ex-wife Elaine, maybe my new wife.  So much has happened in the last several days.  Maybe she wouldn't even want me after this.  There I go thinking too much.

The orderly with a wheelchair came in again.

"One more time, Mr. Corey."

"Are you kidding me?  More brain tests?"

"Yes, I guess they are having a hard time finding out what happened to you.  Five tests are more than the usual."

Here I go again rolling down the halls, and then into the MRI machine.  I got back in time for Elaine to be coming.  My phone started ringing.  I answered it was my brother Wally.

"Hey, Wally."

"How are you doing?"

"I feel good.  Just got back from taking more tests.  I guess there having a hard time finding out what happen to me."

"Really?  As long as you're getting better."

"Yeah, I do feel pretty good.  I'm going to the physical therapy hospital Saturday.  I guess that's good news.  Least that's what they say."

"Yes that is good news.  Oh, Debbie has been trying to call you, but every time she calls she misses is you.  Or maybe she has a wrong number.  She sends her love.  Donny and the girls send their love, too.  Debbie is having her church pray for you."

"I must've have been in one of the test rooms when she called.  If you talk to her again, thank her.  Give my love to all of them.  Wally, Elaine just walked in."

"Say hi to her for me."

We hang up.

"Hi to you.  That was Wally.  I guess I've been missing Debbie trying to call me from Kentucky."

"How are you feeling today?"

"Good enough that they are sending me to Banner physical therapy hospital Saturday.  I guess it's around here."

"Yes, it's where Ruth did her therapy.  It's about a block from here.  So they must think you're doing well enough to send you to physical therapy.  What did the Doctor say about your stroke?"

"They are still looking at the tests.  I did another other one just before you walked in."

"What?  That's five are six."

"I've lost count"

"Everyone at work is praying for you.  Their asking the people in the churches pray for you to."

"No wonder I'm getting better.  Thank them for me.  How are you doing with all this? I haven't even asked you."

"Well I didn't sleep good last night.  I'm tired at work.  But I'll be okay, just as long as you're getting better."
We kiss our little kiss.  A nurse walked in.

"Not again?"

"Yes, I need more blood."

She did her thing and then left.

"I think this hospital is run by vampires.  That is the 8th or 10th time she has taken my blood. Maybe they're having a party for vampires."

We both laughed.  We chatted for a while; just small talk.  Elaine needed to go shopping for food and some other things before she went home.

She said she would stop by and see me Saturday

at the physical therapy building.

"Love you."

"Love you, too."

We kiss a little kiss.

I felt tired.  I closed my eyes and started to drift off to sleep.  There's Elaine and I in our twenties in San Raphael California, 1969.  We're dressed like young hippies.  Elaine's has bright red hair with a leather lace orange top and orange silk pants.  I am in my pin stripe bell bottom pants. We're at some outside rock concert.  The Doors were playing.  We were dancing to the music. Everyone was there. The air filled with grass and I'm not talking about the kind you stand on.

"Mr. Corey, Mr. Corey, wake up for dinner."

There's a nurse pushing at my arm.

"Oh, I was as having a great old dream."

"Sorry I had to wake you, but you don't want cold food."

I half smiled. I'll have to tell Elaine about that dream.
The nurse left and the lady doctor came in.

"Mr. Corey, your doing so good we are sending you to physical therapy tomorrow morning. It's been nice serving you."

"I have to thank all staff here at banner hospital. Did you find out what happen to me?"

"We have so many tests to look over we get behind. Lots of strokes here in Sun City. The doctor in physical therapy will let you know as soon as we know. Best of luck Mr. Corey"

She leaves. I watch TV and about 9:00 fall asleep.

It's Saturday morning, 8:00 a.m. An orderly comes in with a wheelchair.

"Are you ready to get out of here and take one more step closer to going home, Mr. Corey?"

He was nice and friendly. I was already dressed.

"Let's do it. You must take a lot of us seniors over to physical therapy. We have to learn to take it easy at our age. Sometimes we still think we're in our twenties"

We both kind of laughed. I am taken down some new halls, into an elevator, and then to the back parking lot. He helps me into a minivan. In no time we pull up in front of the physical therapy facility.

There's a nurse waiting for me with a wheelchair.

"Here you are, Mr. Corey, take it easy and good luck."

"Thanks."

The orderly helps me get into the wheel chair; a nurse is helping hold things steady.

"Good morning, Mr. Corey."

"Morning to you."

She wheeled me down half a hall way in to my new room.

"You see this yellow card by the door?"

"Yes."

"It means you are new here. The color will change as you get better. We have very important rules here and you have to follow all of them to the letter or you will get yelled that," she said with a reassuring smile.

She helped me get settled in my bed.

"One more thing, we need to test your urine."

"What?"

"A nurse will come in with a little machine to check your urine."

"You mean a cup?"

"No, you will see. Don't go to the restroom. She will be here soon."

"But I have to go now."

"Okay, I'll go get her."

A new nurse came in with this little machine.

"I'm Nurse Johns. I hear you have to go to the restroom."

"Yes."

"You need to go in this cup first, and then I will check you with this wand."

Once I was back in bed she rubbed a little

gel by you know where, then rubbed the wand

around my lower stomach.

As she looked at the screen, she said "That's good, only 30% left."

"What does 30% mean?"

"We will do this two more times.  If your bladder is less than 30% full you'll have passed the test.  It just tells us how much urine you have left after going."

"And that's good?"

She kind of laughed.

"I will explain next time.  Your breakfast is here.  Don't get out of bed for anything if you have to go to the restroom ring us.  Follow the simple rules and will get along just fine.  Your physical therapist will be in here at 10.  Sherry is her name.  Don't forget to use the ringer all times."

The bed next to me was empty.  I was all by myself.  The television's hooked right to the bed.  You just move it back and out of the way.  I decided to turn it on and look for old movies.  The Third Man was on, so I started watching it for the 20th time.  The same nurse came with my breakfast helped set me up.

"Is there anything else you need?"

"No, thanks."

She was all business.  No smile.  Maybe she worked all night.  I eat watching my black and white movie.  I finished just in time.  Another lady came into the room.

"Mr. Corey, I am Sherry, your physical therapist. How are you doing?"

"I'm good."

"Are you sure?"

"Yes."

"Are you ready for little therapy today?"

"Let's do it."

I started to get out of bed.

"Wait until I get a wheel chair."

We went down the same hall way that I came in. Except that instead of going through the front door we took a left into a physical therapy room. All kinds a different equipment; they were balls, mats, stairs, rails and several machines I had never seen before.

"So what's this all about?"

"We want to find out how good your strength is. Let's try some easy things First sit on that chair. Just raise your right leg, now your left leg. The same with your arms. Good now stand. Raise your left leg, stand there for 10 seconds. You did well. Now your left leg10 seconds."
I almost fell over.

"Your left side needs some work. Come over her, try these steps. Don't put your hands on rails. Up and down three steps six times."

I did well on that. i did several more exercises and then I was headed back to my room

"How did I do?"

"Good, two more therapy sessions today with Jonie and Edwin."

"What?"

"The first one is at one today and the next one will be at four. We have to put you through the test here before you can go home. We have to make sure you're okay."

She leaves. It's 11:00 a.m. I'm waiting for

Elaine. No Elaine. They brought me lunch. After that, it was off to my next physical therapy at 1:00 p.m. Maybe Elaine needed to go shopping or something.

Just then Elaine walks in.

"Sorry I'm late. I didn't sleep again last night. I worry was about you. When I finally did get to sleep I did not wake up till ten this morning. Then I had to rush around all morning shopping and paying bills. So, how are you feeling today?"

We kiss our little kiss.

"I already did two exercise routines this morning. Just did more before you got here."

"Oh, that's good. How did you do?"

"Good, I think. I worked with a lady therapist then a young man. They don't say how good you are doing. It's only the first day any way. Maybe it takes time."

"I'm sure it takes time to evaluate you. I'm so tired I could go to sleep here."

I could tell she had been drinking. Her eyes were a little glossed. I didn't say anything. Maybe she needed a drink with all I have been putting her through. Aside from all that, we've been having a pretty good time seeing each other after all these years. Having had a stroke and being in the hospital, who knows what the future will bring.

"I could use a nap myself, come lay with me."

"Are you sure it's okay?"

"What can they say? It's not like we're going to have sex."

We both kind of laughed. I wrapped my arms around her.

"Love you."

"Love you, too"

She fell asleep fast. Maybe my sex days were over any ways I was thinking as I lay next to her. It started fast and ended fast.  What was my life going to be?

I didn't want to admit I had a stroke.  I couldn't sleep at all.  Never could in daylight.  I had to get out of this hospital and test myself.

Inside my heart I was hurting.  I worried that I would not be able to pass all those physical therapy tests.  I was shaky inside.  Kind of faking it but didn't want to say anything. I didn't want to be here two weeks or maybe longer.  She'd been sleeping for a full hour.

"Elaine, wake up am having physical therapy soon."

I had to push her arm a little.

"Oh, I needed that.  What did you say?"

"      "My four o'clock therapy will be in 10 minutes."

Elaine got up and went in to the restroom. About that time a nurse came in.

"Your therapy is running late."

"Okay, thanks."

Elaine came out of bathroom just as nurse was leaving.

"You know, they won't let me go to the bathroom by myself. I feel like a kid. I have to ring for a nurse to go to the bathroom."

"You know, that's probably for your own good. What if you fell over and hurt yourself, or worse?"

"Yes, you're right. That's all I need to do is break my neck."

"You're doing pretty well from last Wednesday. I had the hardest time getting you in the car. I didn't think I was going to make it."

"Thank God you did, who knows what would have happened to me if you weren't there."

"I don't want to think about it. You look 100% better today and it looks like you have no after effects."

"I hope there no after affects...I guess time will tell."

It was a little after four when Sherry walked in. She said Hi to Elaine, we kissed out little kiss, and Elaine said she would see me Sunday morning.

"Will this stuff be harder?"

"You'll find out."

I am back in the wheel chair. Off again, down the same hallway to the left. This is becoming pretty routine. There are three other seniors in the therapy room with me this time.

"I want you to push down on the bike petal 700 times."

"Are you kidding me?"

"You want to go home don't you?"

"Yes, like today."

"Start pushing."

I start counting the repetitions: 100, 200, 300, 400, 500, 600, 645...my legs were about to give out. I was feeling pain I hadn't felt in years.

"Come on, you are almost there: 697, 98, 99, 700. Good job, Mr. Corey. Now your hands. Pull back the handle bar 350 times."

My legs were still hurting. Now my arms and shoulders would be feeling it. But if it'll get me closer to getting out of here I'll take the pain.

"350," I said happily. "Now what?"

"Over here, see these long bar rails?"

They were about 20 feet long and had what I can only say looked like speed bumps inside them.

"Walk over each bump and don't use the rails. Just step over the bump. See if you fall over."

"Oh, thanks a lot."

"Look at me if you start to fall, I will catch you honestly I will."

I surprised myself and actually make it all the way through the obstacle course. I feel very pleased.

"Wait, you to come backward doing the same thing"

"What?"

"You can do it."

My legs already felt like rubber after peddling that bicycle 700 times. I wasn't sure I'd be able to do this I did. Several more different kinds of exercises and I was back in my room. I had to go to the bathroom. They did the gel test again. It was below 30%. One more test to go. And now it's time for dinner. A new doctor came in.

"Mr. Corey, I am Doctor Davis. I hear you

are doing real well on your physical therapy. Maybe you will go home soon. We're still looking over your test results to determine what the problem was. How do you feel?"

"I feel great."

He listened to my heart, checked my pulse, and then looked into my eyes.

"See you tomorrow."

"Thanks, doc."

I was all by myself. I still couldn't believe I was here in the hospital. No less in physical therapy. I shook my head as I thought to myself. What happened to God? How did I end up here? I always took good care of myself. I eat right and exercise.

Things are looking so good between Elaine and i. Even if I don't like her drinking that hard stuff, maybe I could live with it. How many years do I have left?  I'm 72, so maybe 10 good years or so.  I force myself to go to sleep.

It's Sunday morning.  I thank God for saving me and Jesus for what He did.  I was feeling pretty good.  I even felt better in my mind.  I was getting my strength back or was I just kidding myself.  I've heard it said once you have had a stroke you can have another one maybe months from now.

I lay there in my bed thinking about all the things that could happen.  I guess it is all in God's hands, now.  My breakfast is being rolled in.

"Morning, sir."

A new lady orderly with my food enters the room.

"Morning to you and I have to go to the restroom."

"Wait a moment and I will get you a nurse."

"Can't you just watch me?"

"No sir, I just serve the food."

A nurse came in pretty quickly with her she brought the little P machine. She did the gel thing. Checking how much urine I had left inside. Never did ask why. If that makes them happy.

"You passed all three tests. No more tests."

All the while my breakfast was getting colder. Luckily, it was still warm. Two big pancakes, two eggs over easy, and milk. I was watching Good Morning America on television. It was almost over. As I was finished eating a young orderly came into the room.

"Are you ready for some more therapy, Mr. Corey?"

"On a Sunday?"

"Yes, every day is a therapy day.  There are lots of you seniors here keeping us busy.  That's good for me."

"Where is the wheelchair?"

"No chair today.  You're doing so good.  You get to walk today.  You see they changed the card to green on your door.  That means you're doing really good."
"Can I ask you how long you've been doing therapy stuff?"

"Two weeks, I just finished school and I just got this great job right out of school."

"How old are you?"

"I just turned 21."

"That's great, Scott.  It's good to see a young man who knows what he wanted to do and did it."

"Thanks Mr. Corey"

I did several new exercises today and some of the old ones after that I was done. I was back in my room waiting for Elaine.

Elaine came in at ten minutes until 10.  We

said our good mornings had our little kiss.

"The nurses in therapy said I am doing real good for being here only two days.  They are very surprised all of them."

"That's great; maybe you won't have to be here a week or two like most people who have had a stroke."

"Don't say that word; I didn't have one of those things."

Elaine smiled as she walked over to the window she was shaking your head.

"Can you go outside?"

"I don't know let me buzz a nurse and find out"

A nurse said it was Okay to go outside as long as my wife walked with me.  They all think we are married.

"Yes I guess they would, seeing as we both have the same last name.  Why did you decide to keep my last name?"

"As I said on the phone before, I always liked Corey and maybe its fate."

There were three open tables in the patio. We sat at the first one.

"Oh, that sun sure feels good. I did know if I'd ever feel the sun again. I thought my head was going to explode the other day."

Elaine didn't say anything. She always kept

her feelings inside. Even when we were married

back in the seventies, I could tell she wanted a

cigarette but there were no smoking signs

everywhere. She knew better any ways she

worked in hospital half of her life.

"Did you sleep good last night?"

"I sure did, all that physical therapy tired me out. What about you?"

"No, I was up half the night."

"Why?"

"Just thinking about us for one thing. Here we are back together. Now this happens to you."

About that time a mother quail and her babies flew onto the patio.  We drop the subject; it was just small talk anyway.  We held hands just being with each other.  What will happen next? Who knows?

"I guess I better go in my next therapy is soon."

"Okay, I have lots of catching up on house work and some computer stuff from work.  I am so behind I may not be able to come Monday.  I will call if I can't make it.

"That's okay, there's talk I might get out early.  All the therapists are saying I'm doing so well."

She walks me to the therapy room.  As we're going into the room I said, "Maybe you'd better give me your key in case I get out early."

"If you call, I'll come pick you up."

"No, you miss enough work. I'll take a cab it's not that far."

We kiss our little kiss say I love you and I go to therapy did more exercise.

Monday morning, said my prayers to God and thanked Jesus for all He does for us. Had my breakfast, did my morning exercises, and watched television. A doctor walked into the room.

"Morning, Mr. Corey, I am hearing good things about your therapy. All of the therapists are giving you high marks. Maybe you can go home this week. We are still looking at your tests. Your results are hard to define. There are no obvious signs of brain or heart damage, we are still looking, sometimes these things take weeks to figure out. You are looking real good and seem to be doing well. Well, that's about all I have to tell you. I have to go talk with other patients."

"Bye Doc, that makes me feel much better. Maybe I can go home this week."

"We'll see."

The Doctor left the room. Now I was feeling really good. My phone started ringing.

"Hi baby, you at work?"

"Yes, just wanted to call and see how you are doing."

"The doctor was just in, he said I could go home this week, I mean your place."

"That's good news.  You sound real good. Like your old self."

"Thanks, I feel like my old self.  I mean young self."
We kind of laughed.

"I'll try to come after work if I catch up with my book work or I will call."

"Okay, my therapist just walked in."

We said our love you to each other and I hung up.

"Morning, Mr. Corey.  Glad to hear you can walk now.  Are you ready for some really hard exercise today?"

I make a face as if to say "get real".

"Just kidding."

The rest of the day was light exercise, had my lunch. And I watched TV.  A new nurse came in

"Hi, Mr. Corey. I'm Mrs. Olson."

"Nice to meet you.  I've never been called Mr. Corey so many times in my life.  My name is Richard."

"Well Richard, would you like a tour of our facilities?"

"Yes, very much."
"I know you can walk, but we have to use the wheel chair for this tour."

"Let's do it."

I couldn't believe how big this wing was we went down many halls.  There was a nice lounge for the workers with a great big TV room.

"This is all Banner hospital?"

"Yes, Banner is the biggest hospital in Arizona."

"Well thanks for the tour, Mrs. Olson."

"You're welcome; I hear you're getting out today."

"I am?"

"Oh, I thought you knew.  I guess I let that slip.  Please don't say I told you."

"That's great news. I won't say anything."

"The doctor will let you know some time today."

I didn't have to wait too long for the first

doctor to show up.  He talked with me for a little

while, we signed some papers and then they

released me.  All the nurses came in to say

goodbye.  Many of them remarked that I was the

first stroke patient that ever got out of here in less

than three days.  They couldn't believe how fast

my physical therapy went.  All of them were very

happy for me.  They made sure to tell me to take it

easy for the first few weeks.  Make sure I take my

pills and jokingly said they didn't want to see me back here. They did say maybe come by and say hi one day. They were like a bunch of mothers. That was nice. I packed all my stuff then they called me a cab. As a wheel me out four nurses and one doctor were clapping when I went by. What a nice feeling that gave me. It seemed as though they're really did care.

"Thanks a lot to all of you."

There's a cab waiting for me in front of the building with the front door open.

"Hi, sir."

"Hi."
I was on my way home. Actually to Elaine's place. She will be very surprised when she walks in after work today and finds me here.

It was only a short 5 minute ride.

"I bet it's nice to be going home, sir I come

here a lot from Banner with you seniors."

"Yes, it is."

He's a nice young man, maybe in his fifties. We pulled into Elaine's driveway. I try to pay him, he wouldn't take my money. That was nice of him. I look over the neighborhood. What a great feeling to be standing here. I thank God I'm still here and have no bad effects. I know I still was not out of the woods, but time will tell. I went inside, it looked like a castle. So much larger than that little room I was in, it had a new feeling like a second chance of life. Elaine should be home any minute. As I'm thinking that, I hear the garage door open. I wait by the kitchen door. She almost dropped her water bottle when she sees me.

"You're home," she almost yells.

We kiss.

"Yes, they said I was well enough to leave. Only after three days; they were surprised too."

"We have to celebrate. We can go out and have Mexican Food. I know you'll like that."

I was all smiles.

"Yes, all they said was to take it easy for two weeks. I have some pills to get, we can stop at Wal-Mart on our way."

The next two days were good. She didn't

have anything to drink. She was like her old self

we were laughing and having a great time. It was

like the old days when we were much younger. I

was taking my morning walk and Elaine was with

me. Maybe seeing this health issue had changed

her. I was hoping it was true. Friday after work,

she came home and fixed herself a vodka and

seven up.  Now what?

"Don't look at me that way.  It's been a hard week, I need a drink."

"I didn't say anything."

If she only had one drink that might be okay. We both when out onto the patio.  It was all small talk, about the birds, bees, the rabbits and the jets flying over.

"Why don't you have one of your dark beers?"

"Maybe I will."

Drinkers like to have a drinking partner with them.  So I got myself a beer to make her feel good.  I took my time drinking.  She went in and fixed herself another vodka.  Now I was worried. Here we go again.  What next?  Will she be Doctor Jekyll are Mr. Hyde.  We sat there not saying anything.

She went inside for something not sure what it was. I needed to go to the restroom. When I went in to the kitchen she was standing next to the counter.

"What did you do with the two steak knives, they're missing?"

"What knives?"
"Those knives with the black handles, they're missing."

"I don't know what happened to them"

"Yes, you do! Where are they?"

"Maybe the dish washer ate them"

"I'm not kidding! Where are they?"

"Why would I take knives that cost a dollar?"

She started yelling at me calling me names. F this and F that.

"That's the damn vodka talking again," I

yelled back.

"Don't you even say that! I'm perfectly okay."

This went on for 20 minutes. I went into my bedroom and closed the door. I could feel my blood pressure going sky high. I did not need this at all.

The next morning I stayed in my room until she went to work. I had my coffee thinking about what I was going to do. It was great us being back together, but I couldn't take her drinking and my health issues.

That damn vodka. It makes her a different person. I didn't want to be around her when she was drinking.

Here I am in my seventies; I just wanted a peaceful life. I do love her, and wouldn't mind sharing the rest my life with her.  I had to think of

what was more important:  Us together or having

my health.  Having my health had to come first.

And why should she have to take care of me if

something happened?  What if I had another

stroke and was paralyzed.  It brought tears to my

eyes.  God, what should I do?  This tension

between us wasn't good; it was getting to be 9:00

a.m.  I'd made up my mind to go back to

Cottonwood.  I was still questioning myself some

more.  Deep inside I thought I could deal with her

drinking.  That little voice in my head said I needed

to call my brother Wally.


"Wally, this is not going to work for us.  She
likes her vodka more them me.  She's a different
person when she's drinking. That damn vodka can
you take me back to Cottonwood" I said in a sad

voice.

"You mean now?"

"Yes, if you can."

"Sorry to hear that about Elaine.  Yes, I'll be there in about an hour."

I pack my things.  Tears welled up in my eyes.  We had so much history together.  We had a lot to share in our senior years.  When I finished packing I decided to sit at the table and write her a letter.  I wanted to tell her why I was leaving.  It was hard.  Why don't things work out the way you hope?

*Dear Elaine,*

*I am sorry, but I am leaving.  I can't be around you when you're drinking.  That damn vodka makes you a whole different person.  When you are not drinking, I like that person.  I love you, your real self.  I will always love that person and would like to have shared the rest of my life with you.  Now my health is more important for me.*

*Love you always, God bless.*

Tears were rolling down my face.  Wally should be here soon.  I look around at her house then when outside with my stuff and waited on the front porch. I watched all the happy senior couples walking by with their dogs.  I guess I wasn't meant to be happy in this life time.

My cell phone rang. Wally had taken a wrong turn and said he would be here soon it was not much more than a 30 seconds that he pulled into Elaine's driveway.  He had a sad look on his face. We packed all my stuff in his car.  No words were spoken; back on the 101 headed to Cottonwood.

"Sorry things did not work out with you and Elaine.  Connie, I and Nickie really liked her.  She's a real nice person."

"Yes, she is.  But that damn vodka.  I couldn't take it."

"Well, you'd at least tried things don't work out sometimes.  Women are hard enough to understand.  Connie and I have our ups and downs.  God knows sometimes little things just make them mad."

"I know.  This was over some dumb dollar knives that were missing.  She wanted to know what I did with them.  Why would I take anything? I don't do things like that.  God knows, it's that damn vodka talking.  It's happened several times since I've been there.  Sorry about you having to take me back so soon.  I wanted to visit with you guys for week."

"Maybe Elaine will change in the future and

you two will get back together. You remember I had a drinking problem for years. I stopped cold one day. Connie says maybe Elaine will stop because she loves you."

"Well it's all in God's hands now."

We are on I-17, halfway to Cottonwood. We're not saying too much, but just listening to the radio. I closed my eyes only opening them to see where we were from time to time. I did not sleep good last night. We finally got to the turn off onto 260 and then pulled up to my home. We unpack Wally's car and took everything inside. I turn on the television. We sat and had a coke and watched TV for about 20 minutes, again not really saying anything.

"I better get going bro; I have something I have to do today. Sorry it didn't work out for you and Elaine. Love you bro."

89

"Love you too, bro. Give my love to Connie and Nickie."

"Don't worry, things happen for the better sometimes."

"Thanks a lot for being there for me Wally."

"That's what brothers are for."

I watch him drive off by my window.

I was all by myself, again. My insides were hurting. Why does love hurt so much? I just sat there kind of dazed. The TV was on but I wasn't really paying any attention to it. Did I do the right thing leaving like that? Here I am it's was three weeks we've were together and I'm torn apart. It was so nice being with her at first. And now I'm alone again. Why did God bring us back together at all if He knew this was going to happen? Well at least I know I can still love after 30 years by myself.  We even made love four times.  At least I know I am still alive.  I can feel myself going into a depressive state.  I didn't want that after my stroke, so I decided to go for walk.  I stopped at Jack in the Box and had fries and a coke.  I just sat and watched people for an hour or so.  I decided to go to Fry's and pick up a couple of things to eat.  At least I got my mind off those thoughts for a while.  I talked to a couple walking their dog on the way home.  When I got home I didn't feel like unpacking.  I laid in bed listening to the radio trying to get things out of my mind.  I didn't eat anything or take my pills.  I fell asleep.  I woke up around 4:00 a.m. I had turned the radio off sometime during the night. My stomach was what woke me up.

It wanted food and I had to go to the bathroom. The next four days were hard. No phone call from Elaine. I was getting back to my old routine. One day at a time doing the same things I did for the last 30 years. Being by myself and doing those little routine things that we do to try to make ourselves happier. I stop hurting so much, but still have a little depression. I missed her. It was only a few weeks we had together but it was nice that I had some time with her. We shared some very special moments. Just having someone to share things with and be with. I guess it wasn't meant to be. You never know from one day the next. I could have died that day. But here I am. Two more days passed. My cell phone rang. It was Elaine's cell.

"Hi, Elaine"

"Hi, Richard."

There was an awkward pause.

"I miss you," she said.

"I miss you, too," I replied.

"I didn't know I was that bad when I drank vodka. I'm very sorry for being like that. You should have said something to me when you were here."

"I try; remember you said don't say anything about my drinking."

There was an awkward pause.

"I'm very lonely by myself; you think we can try again? I will stop drinking that vodka; maybe just have a wine once in a while."

"You would do that for us?"

"Yes, I can stop drinking any time."

"Are you sure? That's not as easy as you think."

"Yes, no more vodka, I promise!  I would like us to be together.  As I've always said I love you and always will."

"And I love you."

She's crying a lot now.  Her voice was all broken up.

"There's nothing more that I want than us to be happy and be together in our senior years."

"How are you feeling?"

"I'm fine.  It's only been a couple weeks, but I'm doing good."

"You think we can try again?"

"Yes, I'll come back down next week on the bus.  We will talk all week.  I have to go now and do something, love you."

"I love you, too."

We hang up.  I didn't have to do anything.  I just needed to think over what just happened.  My heart was pounding like some lost love.  At the same time I felt good we had talk.

I had talked to my sister Annie and brother Wally about Elaine and I talking again. We talked about her drinking problem. My brother stop cold Turkey one day and my sister has been a recovering alcoholic for over 30 years.

Our father died of alcoholism. None of us wanting that in our lives again, so we all stopped. Life was hard enough without that. They both said maybe she will stop drinking for you and her. But they both also said to be careful. They both gave their blessings. Elaine and I had been talking all that week. She sounded great. I couldn't tell if she had been drinking. She didn't seem to be forgetting what we're talking about or slurring her words. We sounded like good old friends. I wanted nothing more than be together.  We could share the rest our senior years enjoying life.  I pack my stuff again.  I took my camera stuff this time; one of my hobbies.  In my senior years filming dogs with their owners was entertaining.  It was Saturday morning I was on Sedona Airport bus service headed to Sun City.  It didn't take too long to get to the bus stop at the Denny's restaurant in Sun City.  I said a prayer that this time it would work out for both of us.  The bus pulled into Denny's she was waiting there.  She got out of her car and our eyes met.  I could feel the love in them as though we were 20 years old again.  We kiss is as if everything was new.

"Love you Elaine."

"Love you too Richard."

Here back at her house in Sun City, it's a new beginning.

# Part Two

Four days had passed. Everything's going great. We're having lots of laughs going to the malls and having dinner out together. Every night we go for a walk when she comes home from work.

"Hi, I'm not going to ask you about work."

We kiss. She goes off and changes into pair sweatpants. I wait on the patio with some black birds trying to eat her block of seeds.

"Why don't you run that ugly black bird off? That seed is for my mother quail and her babies."

I just raise my shoulders in a halfhearted gesture of "Oh, well". She lights up a cigarette.

"I was at Walgreens today and was checking out that Sunset Bistro. They have karaoke singing tonight we should go and check them out. We could have dinner, too."

"That sounds fun after a hard week of work. People really got on my nerves this week."

"All bosses get to you once in a while. I worked for this lady and she really got too me.  A real ball buster."

We both laughed.

"Have you been to that Greek bistro over there?"

"No I only go to Walgreens when I need something quick"

"You mean you haven't been to the Dollar Tree or any of the little stores at that mall?"

"No, I've been wanting to check them out one day."

I just shook my head.

"You mean in all these years and you haven't really checked anything out?"

"That's not true; I buy most of my clothes form the ladies store, there. Have for years.  I know the owner pretty well.  I even thought about working for them part time if ever retire."

"You should retire you have been working all your life."

She thought for several seconds.

"I guess it's been over 50 years of working. Yes, I should retire."

"That doesn't sound right. Over 50 years of working?"

"Yes, I was a teenager working at the hotel. I'll never forget those English Beatle lads that stayed there. All the crazy girls that came to see them."

"Did you get any autographs?"

"No, I didn't. I didn't even get to see them. I just cleaned their room and it was messy every day."

"Was it a Minnesota winter?"

"I don't remember. That was over 50 years ago. Let's get ready for our karaoke day."

"Sure," I said.

We both laughed.

We dress in our nice clothes and are ready to go out for the evening.

"I always liked the way you dressed.  That pants suit sure fits you."

"Yes, it does."

I pat her on the behind.

"I am ready.  Hey, Jude, Jude, Jude, that's all I know.  What about you?"

"Come on.  I am hungry."

A short drive over to the Walgreen's shopping center.  The little Italian restaurant with an outdoor patio was very busy; all the tables filled with couples.  There's a group of three singing in the front of the restaurant.

There's an open tent over them.  They sounded really good.  We walk over and listened for a while.

"Come on my stomach can't take it I need food" she said.

We walked over hand in hand to the Greek

restaurant patio.  They had one empty table waiting for us.

"Shall we eat outside?" I said.

I could see all the smokers are outside and I knew she was going to smoke.  We sat next to wall waiting for the waitress.  She was out in no time.

"Hi folks, what can I get you to drink?"

Elaine ordered wine.  I ordered a glass of beer.  She orders fish for her dinner.  I ordered a meatball meal.  Everyone is out having a good time.  Most of the people there were our age, seniors.  There was a lot of talking and laughing going on.  You could hear the karaoke singer inside.  They were singing there heart out. Even with the door closed you could hear them.

It looked real busy inside.

"Now this is nice. Dinner under the stars with all these people enjoying themselves."

We lean over and kiss like we use to when were young.

"This reminds me of when we use to go out all the time back in LA." she said.

Our food came out. Everything was perfect. It was very enjoyable being outside.

"When we finish eating we should go in and listen," she said.

"Let's do it."

It was really jamming at the Italian restaurant.

There were people dancing around their tables.

We watch them as we finished eating.

"Let's go in."

"Let me have one more cigarette."

We move over to smoking area. Two other ladies started talking to Elaine. I guess that's what smokers do.  Light up together blowing smoke at each other.  I just listen as they talked and smoked.  Finally after several minutes she was ready to go.  She put her arm under my arm as we walked in.

"Let's stand over there and wait for a table."

It was very small inside.  Just elbow room really.  But it had a nice happy atmosphere.  It's mostly seniors out having a great time with their loved ones.  Just then a lady touched my arm.

"We are leaving you can have our table."

"Oh, thanks."

It was a table in the corner next to a window. We had to carry our drinks inside.  Everyone was having so much fun.

"Let me sign you up to sing with your beautiful voice?"

"What do you want to sing?"

I started to get up.

"Don't you dare, Richard!"

"Come on you have a good voice, Elaine. This could be your big spotlight night maybe there's a big song producer here."

"Richard stop it and sit down!"

A lady MC were running around trying to get people to sing. She was checking the mikes and the sound system and just about then it all completely stopped working.

"I'm going to go outside and have one with my friends. I won't be long."

We kiss.

The MC quickly fixed the problem. Some man started singing an old blue eyes song. We all knew who it was. I look out the window Elaine was in the middle of a group of smokers talking. There was a man and two ladies all of them seem to be having a good time.  This was good for her.  She had been working so hard and not having any fun.  And this was good for us also.

Back together being with someone you love and someone you like being with.  We look good together in our senior years.  We both try to take care of ourselves.  The man sang three old blue eyes songs and he was actually really good.  When he walked by I gave him the Okay sign.  Now a lady looking in her eighties started singing a Barbra Streisand song; I believe it was The Way We Were.  She was real good too. It seems like there are many talented people out here singing tonight.  Elaine walked in.

"You missed ol' blue eyes and he was good."

"Oh, too bad I always liked Frank's music.

But that lady is up there now. I wonder how old she is."

"Well, all I can say is it does not the matter how old she is; she's got more guts than most of us."

We decided to get up and dance. There are people dancing by their tables. We dance to Streisand or at least the song the lady was singing. We were slow dancing like young lovers going back in time. When we were in our twenties we used to dance this way; her head on my shoulder, I was holding her tight. When the song ended I gave her a nice long kiss.

"Thanks for the dance, it's been a long time since I've danced and been out this late."

"Years for me, too. Maybe the last time was when we were married. I really can't remember, but I'm beginning to feel these old bones. I've been up since 4:00 a.m."

"Look a blind lady's going to saying. We'll go

after she is finished."

She sung like an angel.

"Some people have so much talent."

She finished singing and the clapping wouldn't stop.  She was really quite remarkable.

"Let's go, it's almost 11.  All these seniors are night owls."

It only took us a little while to get back to

Elaine's.  We both got undressed.  Got in bed and

made love.  Even kissing like teenagers and

wearing ourselves out.  It was great falling to sleep

with her legs over mine like the young days.  I

woke up at 4:30 a.m. like I always do.  I forgot the

alarm was set.  It went off.  Elaine jumped up

almost falling.  Running to the alarm naked

pushing as fast as she could.  And then the phone

started ringing.

"Sorry," I said loudly.
Now she's running to the phone.

"Hi, hi, no I'm okay. I just forgot, don't send the posse. That's not the way to wake me up."

Now she looked a little embarrassed. She realized she was naked, so she covered herself up.

"Come on we made love last night."

She hurried into the restroom.

"I'll make some coffee while you dress"

"I'm not having coffee this morning. I am going back to sleep I need some more z's."

She came over gave me little kiss.

"See you when I get up. Don't wake me. Have nice big cup of coffee."

I thought maybe I should go back to bed, too. But who was I kidding. Once I am up in the morning, I'm up. I took my coffee out into the patio.

It was cold and dark. No one was stirring, no

cars driving by.  There weren't even birds trying to eating from seed block.  I sipped my coffee as I thought about yesterday.  It was a wonderful night.  Going out to dinner and dancing, listening to some very talented singers who were probably dreaming of becoming stars themselves at one time.  Then coming home and making love to this beautiful lady.  The sun started coming up and the birds started singing. Even a rabbit ran by.  I closed my eyes for a moment.  When I opened my eyes a big coyote was in the yard looking at me.  I stood up and he ran off.  We both kind of scared each other, I think.

Must be time for news, I thought.  My coffee was cold and my stomach wanted something to eat.  I'll see if Elaine is stirring.  Her door was closed.  I opened it quietly and peeked inside. She was in a very sound asleep. The clock read 6:30. I microwaved my coffee, turned on the TV and had fun flipping through the channels. I couldn't find anything to watch. Now wasn't that something? There are 200 channels and nothing to watch. I found 3TV News. That was Elaine's favorite news so I decided to watch some of those reporters.

Some of them have been there for 10 or 15 years and they still looked good. We watch them so much that they have almost become like family members. I need more sleep to, so I lay back down on sofa. I was halfway asleep with the TV on when I heard the microwave oven door close.

"Oh, you're up. What time is it?"

"Good morning, it's almost nine."

"Morning to you."

Did I actually get any sleep, I thought to myself as I was getting up.

"How do you feel, did you get enough sleep?"

"I feel great. Ready for my Sunday TV. I get to watch all my Westerns."

"That doesn't sound fun. I have a better idea."

"Let me have my cup of coffee first."

We both went out into the patio. "It's so nice here in Sun City in the mornings" I said. She lights a cigarette.

"How nice was that going out having dinner and dancing? Listening to seniors our age singing. "They did sound good" she said.

"Did we make love last night?"

"What, what you don't remember? We were great us old farts, still making love." I smiled

"Yes, I remember."

We both laughed.

"We'd better take it a little easier next time. Look above my lip:  whisker burn."

I looked and it was a little red.

"It's not like we're still teenagers." she make face

"Sometimes I feel like a teenager.  You can look in the mirror and you see your age, but your mind still thinks you are young.  It's weird." I raise my eyes

"Yes, I feel the same way.  As they say you're only as young as you think.  So let's think young, but not in sex.  We don't want to hurt each other." she said

We both laughed and agreed.  It so nice us back together again for our senior years.

"I have an idea.  It's going to sound maybe too early."

She pauses for several seconds.

"Well, come on.  What is it?"

"Maybe it can wait for another time."

"Oh, come on Elaine" Get it out there, it can't hurt."

"You move in here with me and we get married again."

She looking into my eyes. It surprised me big time. I was kind at a loss for words.

"That's something to think about in the future. "I said

"That was not a very romantic answer." We have to be sure. With All those years of being by myself and with my health now; there would be a lot of changes. I was not sure I was ready to make them.

She looked away; disappointed

"What's your idea?"
"Annie suggested we visit. Lance and Lloyd. They're kind of expecting us."

"Yes, that would be nice. I can't even remember the last time I saw them. I don't remember Lloyd."

"We can see them today if you want. I'll call first. See if Lance is home today."

"I'm going to take a shower after last night, I hope you are too."

She went in. I sat there thinking. She probably did not like my answer to the marriage question. But with what happened last time I was here, I have to be sure she's really going to stop drinking vodka. Wine, I didn't mind. Over the phone she said she had stopped. However, seeing is believing. It sure would be a nice if we could be together for the rest of our lives. Me, I'm already in my seventies. How many good years do I have left?

That's was always in the back of my mind. I love Elaine. I always have. In fact she's the only lady I ever really loved. Some ambulance is racing by with their sirens blasting. It's probably another senior going through a life changing events. Life

has its moments. Better go in and call Lance to

see if he's home. Elaine was in her bedroom with

the door closed. I peeked in. I embarrassed her

again.

"I'm going to call Lance."

"Okay."

I found my note with this phone number on it
and then called him.

"Hi, Lance, it's me Richard."

"I know who it is, how are you doing?"

"Good, I'm at Elaine's. We would like to
come by and visit you and your brother today if
you're going to be home."

"Sounds good to me."

"Can you call your brother to see if he can
come over also?"

"He always visits me on Saturday and

sometimes we go to a movie. What time were you if thinking of?"

"Around eleven."

"That will work. We can go to a movie later if we decide to."

"Okay, see you around eleven. Oh, could you ask Lloyd if he can bring his guitar? I'd like to tape him playing. See you in a bit."

We hung up. I showered as Elaine got dressed. She's one step ahead of me. I do a quick shave. She still needed to put her makeup on. I was ready to go. I always liked watching her put on makeup. She really does a great job. It makes her look good.

"You dress like a millionaire."

"Thanks, I wish I was one."

"You're doing pretty good for yourself. Nice home, new car. I drive that old tank 86 Lincoln. But I like it. It's a great car."

"Well should we go?  Do you have directions?"

"Yes, I have directions."

We had toast and smoothie for breakfast.

We figured we'd be going out to lunch after visiting,

so we didn't want to have a big breakfast.  It wasn't

busy on the 101 as we were coming up on the

Cardinal's stadium.

"I sure would like to go see a Cardinal's game one day.  I know, I know you're not into football."

"No, I'm not.  But I still like us to go see them play one time."

I just look at everything like a kid in a candy

store.  Phoenix was so big.  Now all that farm land

gone.  There big money for land here.

"Remember when we lived in Phoenix on Camelback in '72.  I had the chance to buy 10 acres in Peoria for $1000 and didn't do it?" I said shacking my head

"Why didn't you?"

"It was so run down and ugly out there in the 70's. Now each one of those acres are going for half a mill. All those 'If we had' in life. If this, if that. Only if we could see into the future."

"I don't know anything about seeing in the future. Seeing all my love ones dying before me. I lost all my family." "Yes that was terrible." "Here comes our turn off." She took a right turn.

Several turns later and we pull up to Lance's house. Just as we stop Lance came out. He must have been watching for us.

"Hi, Lance."

We hug.

"Do you remember Elaine?"

"Kind of. Hi Elaine."

He gave her a little hug.

"Well, let me give you two the tour."

He walked us into each room showing us the

whole house.  It's a man home.  Showing us what

he achieved in life.

"Nice, Lance.  I don't remember your home being so big."

He takes us to the dining room and shows us some pictures on the wall.

"You used to have this big dog.  I can't remember his name."

"Which one?"

"Is your brother coming over?"

"Yes, he is on his way."

"Did you remember to tell him to bring his guitar?"

"No, I forgot."

Just then the front door opened.  Lloyd

walked in carrying a box full of DVD's and some

food goodies.  Everyone said Hi and exchanged

hugs.  I introduced to Elaine and then we all went

into the living room to sit down.

"Lloyd has a great job.  He works for Parks and Recreation.  Not too far from his place," said Lance

"Oh, that sounds fun.  Being outdoors with nature and animals. "Elaine said

"It's okay most of the time.  More work than fun when you deal with people who are not too smart sometimes," Lloyd answered.

"What do you mean?" Elaine ask

"Hikers go hiking and bring one small bottle of water; in the summer heat, in Phoenix.  Not too smart.  I don't have enough fingers to count how many people die because they don't have enough water nor the guys trying to impress their girlfriends that go falling off cliffs."

"Hey, would you two like to see my pictures. I think I have some of you two when you were married from the 70s," says Lance.

Elaine and I look at each other.

"Yes, sure." we both say

"Where did you get pictures of us?" I say

"Mother gave me some several years ago."
"Lance, go get his picture."

"You two were married here... what year was that?"

"1971" Elaine says

"Now you're back together again, that's nice" Lloyd says

"Yes it is nice "I said

"I asked Lance to tell you to bring your guitar so I could video tape you playing for your mother. I wanted to put you on YouTube."

Lance walked in with a big box of pictures.

"Sorry, Lloyd. I forgot to ask you on the phone to bring your guitar."

"That's okay. It would've have been fun." He said with a disappointed look on his face.
"We can do it another time, Lloyd." I say

Lance started pulling out pictures, handing them to us one at a time.

"I don't remember that picture of us." I say

Elaine shook her head no.

"We looked so young and we look like hippies." Elaine says

We both laughed.  Lance kept handing us more and more.  He had some of my sons Todd and Billy.

"Lance I sure would like copies of all these pictures of the boys, Elaine and I."
"Oh, sure.  I'll make you copies one day."

"Thanks, I'd really like that."

We're handing pictures to Lloyd as he munched on chips.

"You guys want some chips?"

"No thanks, we are going out to eat after we leave here."

We visit for two more hours. It was nice to

see them. I hope it doesn't take so long before our

next visit".  It's been almost 30 years, I am thinking

"Your sister Annie sure did raise some men."

"Yes she did, but they had there ups downs; the boys that is."

We were back on the 101. She knows the best Mexican food places.

"What is the name of this restaurant?"

"Abuelo's."

"What does Abuelo's mean?"
"Grandfather."

"What a beautiful day in good old Arizona," Elaine said.

"Sure is. That's why all the snow birds are still coming to Arizona."

I am still looking at everything on the 101. It is hard for me to believe how built up Phoenix has become.

We travel another ten miles on the freeway. She turns off; no idea where I am, and there is no sense in asking. We arrive at the restaurant. The parking lot was full. That was a good sign. Even with all the cars there we were fortunate enough to

find a good close parking spot.

"You're really going to like there food. I've been here many times. I like Mexican food just as much as you and I'm not Mexican."

"You must have some Mexican blood in you somewhere. Did you eat Mexican food when you lived in Minnesota?

"Yes as long as I can remember."

We waited with the other Mexican food

lovers, some of whom were Mexican, and that was

a real a good sign. Everyone had a pager waiting

for their turn to sit down. Elaine was outside having

a cigarette. I just stand and watch people as they

mill about. I noticed a Mexican lady with two little

girls. They always dress them so cute when they

go out in public. In about twenty minutes our pager

let us know it was our turn. We follow the waiters

to the table.

"This place is really packed today", Elaine said.

The waiter asked if he could take our drink order.  Elaine ordered the house special.  That happened to be the large margarita.  I thought to myself, here we go again. I guess will be okay. We are out for a nice meal.  I order a coke.

"It smells good in here, like real Mexican food." I say

There were so many good things on the menu.

"What is good here?"

"Everything, just order what you want."

Our drinks came.  Looking around I could see that all the people were enjoying their food.

"I can't remember if we spoke much Spanish when I was a kid. I can speak enough to get by and half way understand more. I don't remember us kids being around Spanish much. Mother never spoke Spanish. I will have to ask Annie next time we talk"

Our food was being served. Mine was a big

tamale with red hot sauce, rice and beans on a big

flour tortilla. Elaine had some big fancy Mexican

dish.

"Remember that Mexican restaurant in temple city we use to take the boys to all the time. What was its name?"

"I don't remember. We went to so many restaurants way back then."

"Do you hear from the boys?"

I look at her; she can see the sadness in my eyes.

"No, not in years."

That conversation fades quickly. All I want to do is enjoy the moment and that is not a subject I enjoy.

"I don't think I can eat all this. I will have to take the rest home.  Maybe we can have it for dinner tomorrow." Elaine say

"That's a good idea. I am full, too."

She finished her drink.

"I am too full to move and forget about sex!" I say

We both laughed in agreement.

"I will pay for dinner this time."

"No, you won't I am working making good money you are on social security."

"Okay, when I sell a million copies of one of my books I will pay for everything."

We both smile.  Now was the big question. Would she drink more when we get home? Back at Elaine place

"I am going to change into something else."

"Okay, I'll be out on the patio."

I microwave my morning coffee.  I am anxious to

see what happens next.  It seemed like she was in there a long time.  I was about to go in when the door opened.  My heart stopped.  She came out with her vodka glass full.  I must have had that look.

"Don't worry its only water you want to smell?'
I thought it was a dirty trick. She could have used her water glass.

Her phone started ringing. She went in to answer it.  I shook my head.  She was on the phone for twenty minutes.

"That was Donna from work. We talk all the time. She is a good friend."

"That's nice. How old is she?"

"I think she is three years younger than I am."

"That was really good Mexican food and we're getting to eat the rest tomorrow."

"Sunday I am just wanted to stay home and watch my movies. I have to do a load of clothes. Do you have anything that needs washing?"

"No, not now. Thanks for the dinner."

"Sure. Do you like Elvis?"

"Do I like Elvis? Don't you remember when we saw him in Long Beach?"

"Hold that thought."

She went back in and put on an Elvis CD. She turned it up pretty loud and opened the door.

"Yes, I will remember that night forever. We dressed to the hilt. If I remember right, that was one of his last shows, 71 or 72. He was overweight but could still sing his heart out. He was as good as when he was in his twenties."

"Yes you're right. I think he wore his blue jump suit. You know Elaine that is what is good about us back together: all those memories we have from the past, our younger years."

"Yes that is one thing we have. We can almost pick up where we left off. Well kind of. Many years have passed. I am 66 you are 72. I still can't believe we are seniors. I don't feel old, as long as I don't look into a mirror."

We both raise our eyes.

"It's so nice out here listening to the king."

She closed her eyes. I did the same saying a little prayer to myself: Please God, hope this works out this time.

It was almost10 before we knew it.

"I don't know about you but I am tired and going to bed," she said.

"I am right behind you."

I got into bed first.  I was still hard getting

used to having someone else in the bed. We kiss

good night. She is sound asleep in seconds. I stare

at her for a while.  She likes the fan on, the door

opened and the hall light on. I like the door closed,

no fan blowing, and a dark room.  The changes

you have to make when you're in love.  I was about

to go to sleep when she threw her leg over my two legs. I was about get up to get drink of water, but couldn't or else I might wake her. I thought to myself, this is going to be hard to get used to. I don't know if I got any sleep that night. It was sort of off and on all night and I couldn't get up when the alarm went off.

Sunday morning we watch Joel Osteen with our coffee. He really was good this morning. He really packs God's people in by the thousands. God has blessed his family.

"I am going for a walk. You want to come?"

"No, as I said last night, I am watching TV and doing some house work. Don't eat anything. I will fix us eggs and ham."

"Okay, see you in about an hour or so."

We kiss.

"Love you."
"Love you, too."

I lock the front door on my way out.  There are always dog walkers out and about this time of the morning. They really love their dogs here in Sun City. I wave at a lady with her Boxer on the other side of street.  Here I am again walking the streets of Sun City. It was so nice here. Everybody seems to like living here. It was as if I was in a different world and I guess it was in a way. The parking lots were half full at Walgreen's.  I feel good about us. Maybe this time every will work out. I put my hands together as if praying to God.  A second cup of coffee sounded good. There one counter seat waiting for me at Bobby. All the tables were full with all of the local seniors. It must be good food. There is a man reading the Sunday paper next to me. A cute young lady waitress came over to take my order. I ordered a donut and some coffee. I sure would like part of his paper, but he has his nose buried in it. He didn't even look at me when I sat down. I guess he was enjoying his morning and just wanted to be left alone like I do sometimes, especially when I am writing.

I do all my writing at fast food places. There are seniors coming and going all morning. The ladies dress in their Sunday best going to or coming from church. Del Webb and Walt Disney; what dreams they had for mankind, daydreaming as we do. Thank God for giving Elaine and me another chance. It's so nice to have someone to share with and love to be with in my senior years.

The waitress comes over with more coffee.  I decide I have had enough. I look at my watch. It's time for a good walk.  I passed Sun Dial Senior Center.  Lots of cars passing me headed to church or out for breakfast.  I walk this way and that way. I got lost when back the same.  I hurry back to Elaine's.

"I was starting to worry about you.  You've been gone a while."

"Sorry, I kind of got lost. Something sure smells good."

"Good thing you got here now or I would have eaten it all myself.  Come on we'll eating out in the patio."

Monday morning. Elaine is rushing around getting ready for work. It's almost time for her to go. I am watching the news.

"Do you need anything done around here?"

"Yes there's always something that needs to

be fixed.  The front door bell needs fixing. My oven fan works part time. Sky lights need to be cleaned and there is more."

She kind of laughs and shakes her head.

"What are you going to do today?"

"Well, after I fix everything I might go to McDonald's and try to write some more."
"Have to go, running late."

We kiss.

"Love you."

"Love you, too."

Out the door she goes.  I follow carrying her big water bottle for her.  We both tell each other to have a nice day.  I decide I can get a few of her projects done around here, so I took out the bad doorbell and try to fix oven fan but give up on that. I will do it another day.

I walk down Lake Forest Drive, cross at the light on

99th to go to McDonald's on Bell. I try to write today day. I now have three stories going at once. I like walking here. I've been walking all my life. When I lived in Hollywood I'd walk sometimes for five or ten miles. One time I walked all the way to Venice Beach from Hollywood. I took the bus back. McDonald's is full of seniors like me. There are no seats at first, but a man leaves my favorite spot. It is a high seat at the counter. The man next to me said "Hi."

"Good morning, are you new to Sun City?"

"No," he says, "Been here four years. I had to get out those Kansas winters."

"Oh, did you have one those big cattle ranches?" "I said kidding.

"No, I have one of those big wheat farms. My sons are running it now. I really like it here in Sun City. I wish I would have moved here when my wife was still alive."

The conversation trailed off after that. Then my cell phone began ringing.  Saved by the bell.

"Hey, Wally."

"Hi. What are you doing?"

"I am at McDonald's having a coke."

"Remember, I said that Joe and Andranette were coming to Phoenix to visit their daughter? They want to meet us for breakfast this Wednesday."

"Sounds good to me, but Elaine works, so I don't know about her.  I can ask."

"How you feeling?"

"Like my old self almost as if nothing happened to me. I wonder if I really had a stroke."

"What about you. How are you feeling?"

"Connie and I are good. Have to go. Let me know about Elaine."

We hung up.  The Kansas man was about to leave.

"Are you a dog person?"

"Yes we have four on the farm."

He named them all.

"Why did you want to know if I have any dogs?"

"I wrote a book about dogs, Bloodline: The Doberman Family. Check it out on amazon. Thanks. Nice talking with you." I hand him a card

"I will check it out."

He nods his head as he is leaving. I get one of Sun City's newspapers to read.  I see 12 seniors in a group having a good time telling jokes.  My back starts to act up, so I go outside to walk a little. The parking lot is full of nice cars. These seniors must have done well before their retirement years. There were several cars from the 50's fixed up like new.  My back felt better after walking around a while, I go back in and try to write. It will be nice to see Joe and Andranette. I haven't seen them in 35years. I wonder how their kids are doing. There are many seniors moving about. Most have taken care of themselves and are looking good, especially the ladies. Once in while a young person comes in.

The young lady manger, a blonde, is a real hard worker. She seems to like us seniors. A man who appears to be in his fifties joins the 12 seniors and is joking with them. He must be the owner. I look at my watch. I have been here 45 minutes and haven't written one word. As I begin to write a nice looking lady sits next to me next to me. We exchange smiles.

"Good morning."

"Sure is a beautiful morning." She replies and then starts to eat her pancakes. A man joins her and they begin to talking like old friends. I finally got some writing done. People are coming and going. This has to be a million dollar store all because of seniors.

It's time to go buy some goodies at the discount bakery. The bakery was busy with lots of customers. It's the same grouping as McDonald's, mostly all seniors; some young people. I buy some cookies and cupcakes.

I walk around checking out the center. I go into the hardware store. They have almost everything imaginable. It's time for me to go home.

Bell Avenue is busy this time of day. Waiting

on the lights takes too long, so I decide to run across the middle of the parking lot to Starbucks. It is busy there, too. I will have to go there one day. These snow birds really bring in the money. It's nice to meet people from every state, all my age. What an idea Del Webb had. I wonder where he lives. This center has lots of shops for Elaine. There is every possible thing you need within walking distance.  I stop by to see Debi at her Glamor Pet Grooming. I talked to her last time I was here about doing a TV show for my internet webpage (petswelovetv.com). I look in her window. She is grooming a small white dog. Debi is a nice looking lady I her 50's with a spiked hairdo like Elaine's.

"Hi Debi, Remember me?"

She kind of gave me a blank stare.

"I gave you my card about my book and website."

"Oh yes, about a Doberman family."

She finishes her dog grooming then comes over to counter.

"I want to see if you and your shop wanted to do that TV show for pet lover my internet page I said last time we talk."

She thought for few seconds.

"How about tomorrow at The Sun Dial Rec Center? I am going to have a table there talking about the shop and handing out fliers. It's a big event. That would be fine if you wanted to do something there."

"Yes that is a good idea that right by where I live. What time?
We make all of the arrangements.

"Okay, see you tomorrow. Oh, did you happen to check out the website?'

"Yes, I liked it."

She was good at what she did and was busy. Her next customer was waiting on her.  She is a very nice lady and seems to love all the pets that come in for their grooming. I stop at Bell Center for one more look. I couldn't believe how big and nice these centers are just for us seniors. I am very happy walking back to Elaine's.  . It's great to feel happy maybe this time things will work out.

It was getting to be lunch time.  I took my time walking back. I like looking at these homes. Everyone had them fixed differently, but they all seemed to fit together in the neighborhood.  F16's and F35's from Luke Air Force Base fly over. I have to stop and watch them every time. They have so much power. They're gone in no time.  I cross 99th Ave. On Burns Street, some lady was out walking her big white dog. She knows Elaine. We greet each other.

I give her a card. She talks on and on about everything. I tried to tell her I needed to go, but she would let me go. I stopped her for a moment and told her I needed to go to the restroom. She understood that. We said our good byes. It was all that coke I had drank this morning. I hurry off fast. Finally make it to Elaine's. I hope she is not drinking. I hope she is a lady of her word. After I finished in the bathroom, I turned on the TV. I do my favorite thing; flipping through 200 channels looking for something to watch. I went in to the kitchen, made a beef sandwich and added a handful of chips to the plate. I'm still flipping through channels when she walks in.

"Oh, off early?'

"Yes I wanted to come home so we could go shopping at Wal-Mart."

We kiss.

"That sounds good. You know I like seeing new places."

She went into her room and changed. Off we went to Wal-Mart.

"I have to show you something bad."

"What's bad? "

"Just wait."

As we turn down the next street I see what she is talking about. There was a home that had burned to the ground. It looked so out of place here in Sun City.

"Was any one hurt?"

"I don't know," Elaine said kind of teary eyed "There's nothing left."

Lots of cars driving by looking at what they never wanted to see at their homes. We went back to 99th and then on to Wal-Mart.  The store was very busy always is. Here's was another man with a big idea.  Wally World.  They almost own the whole world.  People like to buy cheap things even if it is from another country I was thinking. She sends me off to get some things. When I return, I have a hard time finding her. These stores are as big as 10 football fields.  Finally, I find her. She is looking at clothes.  She tells me she will probably be here a while so I go look at man's clothes. As I am headed to the man's section, I notice a couple chatting about kid's clothes.  I find it interesting to watch people sometimes. Then I remember; I forgot to tell Elaine about Joe and his wife coming to town. I forgot her name. 30 years is a long time. I will tell her when we get back to her place. When I come back she's still looking at sexy panties.

"I can't find what I want." She'd been there over half an hour.

There are millions on the racks, but I don't say anything. We men know better.

Two hours later and her basket is full of food stuff.

"Your basket over full has to be $100 worth of food in there."

"Where have you been?  More like $250."

"Are you kidding?"

"Wait and see."

The lady cashier had a weird hairdo. She looks to be in her 50's.  We unload our cart onto the counter.

"Does your husband like your hairdo? "I asked her.

She just looked at me kind of funny as does Elaine.
"I never asked him."

She laughs and we join her. Elaine's face is as red as her hair.

"Leave it up to you."

"Well you don't see a pink Afro every day. I had to say something."

She just shook her head.

"Did you see the food bill? $225. That's what you pay for full basket today."

Now I am shaking my head wondering how a family of four makes it today.

We are back at Elaine's putting food away.

"I need a drink and a cigarette."

I was kind of surprised me when she said that. She gets a big glass of water and we go out onto the patio.

"I have some news.'

"Oh, you do. What?

'Wally called me when I was at McDonald's this morning. Do you remember Joe and his wife I forget her name do you?"

"Sure I do its Andranette She's the person that introduced me to artichokes."

"You remember that after 30 years?"

"Yes, that's the time we went over for dinner. She served artichokes and she showed me how to cook them.  Now they are one of my favorite foods."

I am shaking my head. Unbelievable what we remember.

"Anyway, they are going to be here in Phoenix and want to meet us for breakfast."

"That's nice.  I'd like to see Andranette and thank her again for showing me artichokes."

"There's more. They want us to meet on a week day when you work."

"Don't worry, I can take any day off I want. The boss owns me all kinds of days off. I've never had a real vacation in 12 years. When will they be here?"

"Wally has to call me and let me know, maybe Wednesday or Thursday."

Next two days she came home from work. She looked tired and was always hurting. She has two glasses of white wine. Her back is hurting so I give her a long back rub.

"You know you should really retire. If you don't like your work and it makes you hurt everyday it's time to leave."

"Yes, I know. But I am worried I won't make enough money to pay for this house, the association and the upkeep."

"Well you need find out. Call social security. They will let you know how much your retirement is going to be. Better than coming home every day hurting like you do. Your health should come first."

She was kind of going to sleep so I stop rubbing her back. I just sit and watch TV, lowering the sound so she can rest. It was almost 830pm when she woke.
"Why didn't you wake me? Did you eat

anything?"

"No, I was waiting for you."

She jumped up and hurried into the kitchen to fix something. This is the time she eats every day. It's a late dinner.  That something I have to get used to.  If I eat late I can't sleep very well. I don't say anything. It is her home and her ways, I am just a guest. It is 9:15 p.m. when we eat. I am already sleepy and now I am full. It is past my bed time.  It is hard getting use to other people's ways.

"I am going to sleep. "I say

"Me, also."

She laid down on the sofa; said it was better for her back. We kiss and say our good nights and love you's. I sleep in her bed.  It feels funny, her on the sofa and me in her bed.  I look up to God and tell Him thanks. I am sure it will take time to get use to each other.  It is nice to have someone to love in you senior years.  I go into a deep, deep sleep. I dream Vodka is being poured all over me. I can't get away. Someone is laughing in the back ground lighting a match. Then I hear the bathroom fan go on and it wakes me up. That was a weird dream. What does that mean? She opened the bedroom door.

"I was hoping you were awake. I need my work clothes. I have some coffee going."

"Good, I need some."
I didn't say anything about the dream.

I pick up her things off the sofa.  Then straighten the room up as she gets dressed. I Fix myself a cup of coffee, and then take my little hand radio out onto the patio.  I like to listen to KFYI in the morning.  The birds are waiting for her to

remove bucket from the bird seed block.  It is her

thing so I let her do it. One of her neighbors comes

and does something to his air conditioner.

Elaine comes out and the first thing she does is light a cigarette.

"All of your bird friends are waiting for breakfast."

"Oh, why didn't you move the bucket?"

"I just figured it was your thing and did not want to intrude."

She removed bucket and we didn't not have to wait long for the first birds to appear.

"You sure are lucky to have such a nice place to wake up for very day."

"Yes, if only I didn't have to go to work.'

"Well that's up to you. Only a phone call away from Social Security."

"I will call them after work today and find out

how much money I have earned after 50 years of working."

"You must miss all you family.  No one left."

"Yes I do very much."  Her eyes tear a little. "Was your father an alcoholic all his life like my father?"

"Yes. Poor mother had to live with his alcohol binges all her life. I had to leave when I was a teenager to live with Aunt Ruth. They were always fighting.  I don't want to talk about it anymore. They were loving parents in their last years. That's how I want to remember them. I have go running late again."

We kiss.

"Love you."

"Love you, too.  See you after work."

Now, what shall I to do? Watch news or go for a

long walk.  I decide to go to the Walgreen's Center

and write.  Those outdoor restaurant patios are

nice and comfortable. I take my tote bag full of note

books.  I pass out cards to all the friendly dog walkers around. Thank God I had this book and web site going.  They keep me busy in my so called golden years. I guess they are in ways.  I do what I want. Come and go as I want. Now I have Elaine back in my life.

What more could a man ask for?  I didn't have any bad affects from the stroke. Thank God life is good.

I walked to Walgreens Shopping Center. Seniors everywhere, doing all kinds of shopping.  I just want some place to sit outside.  The Greek Restaurant patio looked to be the perfect place to write.  I went inside the gate.  There was a big empty table just for me, now this was nice. I sat watching retired seniors coming and going from Walgreens, no doubt doing big business with prescriptions. Yes, I am part of that group.

I now take pills for my stroke as well as other things. I sat there thinking. I am back here after what happened last time?

"Love, love, love, we all want to be loved", I said to myself shaking my head. I looked up to God thinking you brought us back together again. I hope you know what you're doing. I wrote for about an hour. As I was walking over to hardware store my cell phone began ringing.

"Hey, Wally."

"Just got a call from Joe. He wants us to meet him for breakfast in the valley Thursday. Can Elaine get off work?"

"She said she can get off any day she wants"

"Good Joe will call me and let me know which restaurant. He said he would try to pick one kind of in the middle for all of us so we don't have to drive twenty miles each."

"Okay, let me know that will be great seeing them now we are in 60s and 70s. So, so what else is going on?"

"Just taking Connie to the doctor for her feet"


"How are things going there with you and Elaine?"
"She is doing good. No damn vodka. Vodka and her temper don't mix.  Only a wine, which is okay. She doesn't go bananas."

"Have to go. Connie and I are saying a prayer for you two."

"Thanks, love you bro."

"Love you, bro."


I go into hardware store buy three V-neck t-shirts. They are red, black and blue.  They are on sale.  I decide to take the long way back to Elaine's place.  I see a big coyote looking for food.  Wonder if it is the same one that was in our yard? You have watch out for them trying get your dog Elaine says. I take my time, waving at other walkers as we pass.  There are a lot of them out walking with their dogs.  I get back home and decide to have some of cookies and milk.  I pull my easy chair back almost like a bed and turn on an old cowboy movie. My eyes are about to close.  I hear Elaine pull in to the garage.  I shake my head a little to wake.  I go to meet her at the kitchen door.

We kiss.

"I won't ask about your day."

"Don't."

"Wally called."

"Tell me outside."

She gets herself a glass of wine.  I hold open the patio door and follow her outside.  She lights up her cigarette. Now she is ready to talk.

"What did Wally say?"

"Thursday morning he would like us meet

them for breakfast.  Can you get off work?"

"Yes, I can."


It was kind of strange us not talking about what happened last time I was here,  about why I left and about her going off the deep end when she drinks that terrible vodka.  She said on the phone in Cottonwood she would not drink vodka any more. I was going to say something.
When I looked over her eyes were closing.  She works with a computer all day, I am sure she needs to rest. I got up and walked out to the bird bath.  It needed water so I filled it up.  As soon as I sat down, a black bird that was waiting for water jumped in and got a drink.

"Sorry I am such bad company but my eyes

are burning."

"One way to solve that, retire. Let me get your eye drops"

She puts couple drops in each eye.
"It will be nice seeing the Wally and Connie." I say.

"Yes getting a day away from work will be nice too. I feel like big fat In & Out burger with fries. How does that sound to you?"

"My mouth is already tasting it. Only this In & Out is so hard to get into."

"How hard can a drive thru be?"

"You just wait and see."

"Where is it?"

"Not that far off Bell Avenue."

She finished her wine. We get up to go in. I

pat her butt. We kiss a long kiss. We go and get

our burger and fries and bring them home. We

watch a little TV together. I notice she is already

dozing off. It is a long day when it starts at 4:30 a.m. in the morning. So I watch some more TV. She goes to her bed room and falls asleep with her street clothes on. I put blanket over her. It is past 9:30 p.m. and my eyes start to droop, so I get up and do my bathroom things.

I join her in bed laying there thinking this was so nice being with Elaine, watching over her. She is cooking meals for us. Who would have thought we could be back together again after the last time. I felt real good inside. All I wanted was to love her and be loved back. Don't we all? I thank God, say a little prayer and fall to sleep.

Thursday morning we are on our way to go have breakfast. This was a special day as we were going to visit with a couple of long lost

Estrada's, Joe and Andranette. Wally and Connie were on 101 heading west. It's a nice morning. We passed the new Indian casino. The city has been fighting with them since they decided to open. But it will open before Christmas.

"Won't it be great seeing Joe and Andranette? What I mean, you losing all your family. Now you have a new family in your life, my brothers and sisters and all of their children right here in Phoenix. All a short drive from Sun City."

"Yes that is great."

"Do you remember about the Corey's and Estrada's; the two brothers and sisters that married each other?"

"Oh, that's right I do remember a little. It's going to be nice to see all of them."

I didn't know where we were, but Elaine did. She knows her way around

Phoenix pretty well.  She took exit 42 off the freeway onto some street I did not know.

"That restaurant should be right here.  Let's see those directions."

"I'll call Wally."

We pull into parking lot while I get a hold of my brother.

"Wally, tell Elaine where to go."

She just shook her head with a sly grin. Wall told her it was only two more blocks up the street we were on.  She gets her bearings and within a few minutes we pull into the restaurant parking lot. Everybody is out front waiting on us: Wally, Connie, Joe, and Andranette.

Everyone has a big smile, hugging each other as families do. All the ladies dressed so pretty.

"Joe, you look good. You too, Andranette. You too, Wally and Connie."

Wally pats my back. The ladies were already together as we go in.  They have a table waiting for us. The place is packed on a weekday. We have a table in the far corner to ourselves.

"I don't know about you guys, but I am hungry." Joe say

Joe sat and Andranette sat in the middle so everyone was close and could talk to both of them at the same time. We all ordered coffee.  The ladies were talking away; they had a lot of catching up to do.  My stomach is trying to embarrass me by making loud noises. Wally is talking to Joe, but I can't hear them because they are facing away. Andranette is talking to Connie.  Elaine is having the same problem because she is on the far end next to Wally.

"Andranette, how are your girls doing, I mean young ladies?"

"They're doing just great. Jules works for Disney and Jesse works for a big entertainment company. I have beautiful a grandchild we enjoy as much as we can."

"That's great."

I was hoping she wouldn't ask about my boys. Just then, Connie asked her something. I was saved by Connie.

"So, how are you doing Richard after your stroke?"

"Just taking it easy for a while, Joe. Doing what the doctor says. That was a real scary thing to go through."

"Tell me. I don't know if you know I had a heart attack last year?"
"No, I didn't hear. You're looking real good."

"Thank God, not bad for 75 now. I can enjoy my little sweet grandchild. Oh, before I forget, we bought your book about the Dobermans the other day. We really liked it."

"Thanks. Did your grand kid read it? It is a

good book for kids."

"No, not yet. I will try and remember to give it to her. She likes to read and reads pretty well for a six year old."

"Well, give it to her when you go back home."

"Yes will make a note of it."

Wally was asking him something. It was 30 minutes and we were still waiting for our food. It was super busy there, I am sure they had a lot of orders to deal with.

It was 15 more minutes before our food was being served. We all of stopped talking to eat. There was lots of food to eat. After we ate, Connie took a group picture of us. It felt good to be part of a family again. Living in Cottonwood all by myself; I did not get a chance to see these guys very often.

"Say Joe, I did hear you and Andranette had

very good fortune finding out she is part Indian and is now was getting income from a tribe."

"Yes, we did. That is helping us buy a fixer up in the hills. That should keep us busy for a while. You and Elaine will have to come to California and visit us."

"Yes one day."

The small talk continued for almost two hours.

"Do you think we'd better leave? We have been here for over two hours," Andranette said.

We all agreed we had been there a long time. As we all started to pay our portion, Joe insisted that he and Andranette pick up the tab. We all thanked them.

"Say Joe, don't forget to call Annie. She's been cleaning house all week and making special foods for you guys."

"Oh, I will. We are going to Sedona first, and then we will go see her."

"Oh good, it is only one hour from Sedona.

We all talk in in the parking park lot for

several more minutes. Connie came over to me

and said she was really happy for Elaine and me

and that she hoped it worked out. I thanked her

and we hugged.

"Let's get back together again." Joe said.

As we all say, only God knows if that will happen.  Back on our way to Sun City

"Now wasn't that nice being part of a family again? It has been a long time since we were together." Did you say thing anything to Andranette about the artichokes?"

"Yes, but she didn't remember that day.  I guess it only affects the person it has happened to."

"Did you enjoy yourself?"

"Yes Connie and I talked.  We get along real well. Andranette and I were showing off our diamond rings.  Mine were bigger."

We both laughed.

"We should go do something it's almost 2

o'clock."

The car radio was playing The Beatles, Hey Jude. I started singing. Elaine joined in. We were having a good time.

"We need singing lessons." Elaine said.

"I was thinking it would be fun it we took dancing lesson at Arthur Murray's." Elaine said.

"The one by your home? I am open for anything at my age. Let's do it. I can check the cost next time I go to McDonald's."

"Would you like to see more of Sun City?"

"Sure."

So we dove around Sun City for a few hours. We went by the dog park.

"I will have to come here and tape some of these dogs if I can use your car one day."

She didn't say anything.

"Do you know anything about that gas station next to True Value? They sell used cars. I've been looking for a good used car that doesn't cost a fortune."

"Yes, I use that station all the time. They are nice to us seniors. They don't take advantage of us. Very honest."

We ended up back at Elaine's.
"I feel like a nap" she said.

We both undress. Lying in her bed, we begin kissing and making love. This time acting more our age; holding each other.

"I love you, Elaine."

"I love you too, Richard."

Elaine falls asleep. I am halfway asleep when my phone rings in the other bed room, so I get up to answer it.

It is my doctor from Cottonwood calling about my appointment next week. I ask them to change it to the end of the month. Things were going so good here I didn't want to end it. It was like a whole new life was opening up for both us. She was a lady of her word. No vodka for several days. Wine was okay.  I watched TV in the nude like in the old days when the boys were in school.

"Did you forget something?"

"What?"

"Your clothes, that's what."

"Don't you like seeing my muscles?"

"Yes, Mr. Atlas."

We both laughed. I got up and dressed. She went outside on the patio to smoke.  I went into the kitchen to get a 7-Up and join her outside.

"So, you are looking for a used car here? Why don't you buy a truck with a camper?  We can go camping.  I always wanted to see the USA."

"Me, too.  Something to think about seeing the USA with someone you love."

We kiss. She tastes like cigarettes. Yuck, the things you put up with when you are in love.

"That would be fun seeing all America.'

"I'd say, even if we saw part of America. It might take years to see all those states. Then I would have to retire for sure."

"There is a good reason for you to retire."

"Here's something else to think about. What if we got remarried?"

It kind of surprised me again. I didn't know what to say.

"Cat got your tongue?"

We both laughed.

"I sure like this taking a day off. Maybe I won't go back to work for the rest of week. I will just take a long weekend."

"Won't the boss get mad?"

"She owes me 12 years of days off."

She went back to work Friday. We cook together just like our younger days back in 70's and 80's. We always did everything together. Now it seemed we were doing it again. It was like time got turned back except we were in our 60's and 70's going on our 80's.  Time was good to us kind of. We were having fun laughing lots. Talking about the old days when we dressed alike. We both had white jump suits in those hippie days, dancing to disco music under all of those flashing lights. Just having fun with someone you love. Now here we were together. She is basically the same to me to after all these years.

"You did it God," I said to myself.

Saturday morning.  She always watched her cowboy movies on Saturday.

"I am going for a walk. I might go to McDonald's for a coffee."

"Okay, but don't eat too much.  Let's go out to brunch for some Mexican food."

"Okay, that sounds good. See you around 1."

We kiss.

I walk down 99th Ave to the Bell Center. The lot was half full of seniors keeping busy doing what they like even on Saturday. Traffic was like a week day. I waited at the light several minutes. Finally, it turned green. 38 seconds to cross I make in 10. McDonald's was busy as usual. My favorite seat was taken, so I waited for a nice looking senior couple to move. It did not take too long. I wrote something new today. The first page had coffee with cookie on it. My watch was saying it was time to go as was my stomach. I could taste the Mexican food, already. I walk back fast. I counted 20 golf carts on my way back.

"I'm back."

Elaine does not answer and I don' see here

anywhere inside.  I think to myself she must be out on the patio. Just then she walks out from her bedroom.

"Woo Hoo, you're already dressed. You look nice. I should change into something nice, too."

"You look fine and I could eat a bear. Let's go."

"Can I have half of your bear?"

We jump in the car and head west.

"Did you get any writing done?"

"Yes I did but it's a surprise."

"Surprise? Why would it be a surprise to me?"

"Will tell you at the restaurant."

"Oh, good you know I like surprises.  By the way, we are going to Garcia's on restaurant row."

She turned here and there.  Good thing she knows where she was going.  Every restaurant brand name was there.

"Isn't this kind of where the Diamondback Spring Camp is?"

"Yes, over there." She points out passed the parking lot. Garcia's was parking was full. It looked as though all of the restaurants were busy.

"I can't believe how busy all these restaurants are."

"Snow birds and Phoenix has a million of them."

Even with the crowds, we didn't have to wait for a table. We got a nice middle booth. We both ordered combination plates. These plates were loaded, even came with beans and rice. Elaine ordered a pitcher of champagne.

"So what's this big surprise?"

"Well I was sitting at McDonald thinking about us. What a great love story this would make. Here we haven't seen each other in all these years. All the things that happened last time when was here Oh, by the way how come you haven't ask about my stroke?"

She takes a big drink.

"Because you look great."

Nothing else was said. Our food was being served. We began eating.

"What about this story?"

My mouth was full of food, so it took me a second to respond.

"You hear about these love stories all the time: a loved one finding their lost love after 25 or 35 years, just like us. So, I am going to write our love story. I'm going to call it, A Senior Love Story, Love Never Dies."

"How are you going to write it?"

"Just the way it's happening, the true story. I only have one page. That is what I wrote at McDonald's this morning. I repeated it."

The conversation trailed off. We got busy eating, drinking and watching people.

"This Garcia's is really had good Mexican food."

I had one glass of Champagne, she almost finished the pitcher.

"What should we do, now?" She said.

"Let's go to a movie in the Arrowhead Mall right over there, I'm buying."

"No, I don't feel like a movie. I feel like taking a nap after all that food."

So we go back to her place with our left over Mexican food.  I go into the restroom and when I come back out there she is fixing herself a drink; vodka.

That terrible feeling comes back over me again.

"Don't look at me that way. I am only going to have one."

"You said you wouldn't drink vodka anymore."

"No, I didn't. I never said that."

I just shook my head; here we go again.  I

went into the living room and turned on the television She when outside with her vodka.

A little while later she came back in and fixed another drink. I couldn't believe after all the great times we were having.

"I can drink what I want. It's my house you can leave if you don't like it."

She was trying to start a fight.

"You need help with your alcohol."

"Fuck you, I do not."

She stormed outside, slamming the patio door as she went. I could feel my blood pressure rising sky high. I went into the guest bedroom, closed the door, and lay on the bed with tears in my eyes.

I had some crackers in here. That was my dinner. I didn't sleep half the night. I wasn't going to stay here with her going back on her word. I hated that damn vodka and what it did her. A nice lady controlled by the devil drink. How can a person change from one day to the next day? How can she completely ignore that someone loves her and wants to live the rest of their senior years with her. I lay there thinking all these things. It was 2:00 a.m. I better try getting some sleep. I didn't have any more tears to cry. I don't know if I slept or not. The sun was coming up I felt worn out. Maybe it was my age or that stroke I just had. Her bedroom door was closed. She forgot to set the alarm, good. I check my blood pressure 180 over 145 not good at all. I just sat sofa in the den, half asleep.

She came out and didn't even look at me.

She went straight to the patio.

"Elaine I am leaving. I am not staying here with you drinking like that."

She didn't even turn and look at me. I went into the guest bedroom and packed everything for a second time hoping my brother Wally was awake. He is retired so sometimes he sleeps in. His phone rang several times. I figured he was still sleeping. Just about the time I was going to hang up:

"Hello."

"Wally?"

I paused for several seconds.

"Wally, can you come pick me up and take me back to Cottonwood?"

There was even a longer pause.

"What am I having a bad dream? Not again?"

"Yes she started drinking that damn vodka, again. I am packing my stuff."
"Okay, after I eat breakfast; about an hour."

"Thanks. See you out front with my stuff."

I carried all my things out front. She didn't come in at all. She had been out there almost two hours. I guess smoking ten cigarettes. My cell phone rang.

"I am almost there."

"Good, I am out front."

We put everything in his car and got ready to go. As we were backing out of her driveway the front door opens. She just looked at us, and then closed the door.

We didn't say anything to all the way out to the I-17 freeway. Maybe he was mad having to do this again, driving me back to Cottonwood, a 250 mile round trip for him. I could not blame him.

"I am not doing this again for your love life. You have to buy yourself a car."

"You won't have to. It's over. She likes her vodka more than us being together. I can't put up with that."

"She has a drinking problem she is an alcoholic."

"She doesn't think she is an alcoholic."

"That's the first thing you do. I was an alcoholic, just like dad and Annie, but I stopped on my own."

"Me, too."

"It's up to her to take the next step; AA"

"She will never go to AA. She would kill herself first."

"That's a shame. Connie and I were so happy so happy for you two. She really liked Elaine."

On our way back to Cottonwood we didn't talk too much. He could tell I was hurting inside my heart and he probably wasn't too happen doing this again. We just listened to car radio.

We were headed down the grade into Camp Verde. I was trying to catch a little sleep closing and opening my eyes all the way.

"Do you want to stop and get something to eat at Burger King?" I said.

"No I have to get back. I have things to do today."

"What things?"

"Take Connie to the doctors, lots of things" He said in an unhappy tone.

After ten minutes on the 260 we were pulling into my small town of Cottonwood my place. We unpack.

"Do you want a coke before you go back? And here's 40 dollars for gas."

"No, that's okay."

" No, take it. Thanks again."
"I am sorry bro it didn't work out for you and Elaine. I know you really care for her."

We hug and then he left. I flop on sofa. Tears came to my eyes. I just sat there for the longest time wondering why things didn't work out. All I want is to be happy. Is that too much to ask God? I lay down and close my eyes.  I was tired.  I did not sleep well last night.  I woke up once in a while looking at the clock. I did that all day. The sun was going down and I hadn't eaten all day.  I just did not feel like eating.

My stomach didn't care what had happen

today. It wanted food. I look in the icebox. Not much there.

I had been gone for almost two weeks. So I had a can of V8 and watched the news. I made me more depressed. I tried to watch Bones, Elaine's favorite. There are too many dead bodies. I looked for something funnier. My body felt drained. It was 7:30 p.m., so I decided to go to bed. My cell phone started ringing. I wasn't going to answer it, but then decided it might help me think of something else.

"Hey, Wally."

"Just called to see how you were doing.

"I am okay."

"You don't sound okay. You sound really down."

"That's because I didn't sleep last night."

I lied. I was very depressed.

"Connie and Nickie say Hi."

"Thank them. I have to go to the bathroom."

I lie again. I didn't feel like talking.

All night I tossed and turned. I woke up at 3 thinking about us. Why is love so hard? It's the only thing God give us that doesn't cost anything. Or, does it? We all want to be loved and give love. I am looking up to the ceiling; God why did you bring us together if you knew this was going to happen?

I close my eyes trying to force myself to sleep. It worked somewhat. 6:00 a.m. lying there now trying to force myself to get up and eat something. I thought about calling my sister, Annie.

"Snap out of it Richard "I yell at myself.  I get up, make some tea and toast. Open up my computer 1000 emails.  It takes an hour to delete them all.  I check the clock; sis should be up so I rang her number.

"Hi sis, I am back home it didn't work out."
"Oh, I am so sorry to hear that."

 "She liked that damn vodka more than us."

 "I thought you said she said she would stop drinking vodka?"

 "She did over the phone and she was good all the time I was there.  She started again yesterday."

 "I know that's the way alcoholics are. She needs to go to AA like I did 33 years ago."

 "She will never do that. She's like her father off and on.  She knows what her mother went through."

 "Yes, it's hard, I know. Maybe you're better off without her. Sometimes I wish I hadn't called her and put you through all that."

 "Don't say that. It has nothing to do with you. Everything has a reason they say."

"How did you get back?"

"Wally, again."

"What a great brother we have."

"Yes, he's always been there for me."

"So, what happened this time?"

"The same thing. She was real good, didn't drink for several days.  That damn vodka. We were having a great time.  Doing things we both enjoyed, lot of laughs.  It was nice us together.  We go out to brunch, have champagne and that does it. She comes home and starts drinking that stuff. It changes her from sweet Elaine to mean nasty Elaine. If she could only see herself the way I do. I can feel my blood pressure going sky high so I go into my bedroom and stay there until the next morning. I call Wally.  Now here I am all bummed out."

"So sorry for you. You know the last time I tried to talk to Elaine about my AA, she didn't want to hear it.  I was going to send her some information but she didn't want any. She said she is not an alcoholic. You can't do anything unless they want help and admit they're an alcoholic. So, how are you doing?"

"Well, I am okay. It just hurts. When you hope things are going to work out this time.  We have so many things in common.  We have a great history together. So many things going for us. Then that damn vodka ruins everything."

My voice starts to crack and my eyes begin to fill with tears. There is a long pause.

"I am so sorry Richard you had to go through that."

"Oh, I'll be okay. It is just going to take time. Thanks, sis for being there. I will be okay.  I have to get something eat.  Talk to you again.  Love You, Sis."

"Love you, brother. I will say a prayer you."

I sit there shaking my head. Why, why, why don't things work out the good way?

Two weeks go by and I do not hear from

Elaine.  My life was getting back to normal.  I was

driving to the post office this morning and I see a

man just putting a sign on car for sale in front of his

home. I stopped and asked about the price.

We go back and forth on the price, but can't agree on anything. So I start to walk away when he stops me and we agree on my last offer.  It's a very nice 2007 Hyundai. Something finally went my way.

Now I can let my old 86 Lincoln rest.  I call Wally and Annie and tell them about my new car. They were happy for me.

Now I can visit them as often as I would like.  Now, I have to get back into the world. Two more days pass.  I am test driving my new car.

I stop and say hi to Lauren see if she would like to go dancing Friday at the Main Stage. I always liked her. Her car is not at her place, so I leave my card and a note for her to call me.

Thursday morning at 6:30 a.m. and I am on my computer deleting emails when my cell phone starts ringing. I answer it thinking it was Wally or Annie. Instead I hear a loud crying voice. It was Elaine crying her heart out. She says I can't take it anymore and that she needs my help, to please help her. She has been drinking that vodka all day for weeks.

Drinking it straight is killing her. Please help. Can I come to Sun City? I listen to her for twenty minutes begging me.

"Yes, I will if you are ready to stop drinking."

"Yes, yes, I promise. Can you come today?"

"No, tomorrow. I brought a new car. I will be there tomorrow."

She sounded real bad. Her voice all shook up.

"Don't drink any more today Elaine. You have to pray to God for help."

"I will, I will."

We talk for 45 minutes. I try to assure her with God and AA she can stop drinking, but it is mostly up to her. She agrees to everything.  She just wants me to come down and be with her. After we hang up, I sit there thinking maybe this is it. She sees what can happen to her and she wants to stop. Maybe we can have a life together. Maybe that's why I just got this car. Maybe a part of God's plan? I pack all day all and I am excited again.  I don't say anything to Annie or Wally about what I am about to do.

Next morning I call Elaine to let her know I am on my way.  I should be there in about two hours.  It's 9:00 a.m. as I enter on I-17 past Camp

Verde.  The new car is running great. Zooms like a

sports car. Everything works nice.  Almost two

hours, now I am at the101 freeway heading west;

not too busy.  I take the exit off on Bell Road.

It is only a matter of minutes before I am pulling
into her driveway. I sit there for several minutes

hoping this is for real.

Even say a little prayer. I knock on her door.  She

gives me a little kiss.

"Thanks for coming."

It's not like it was the first time I came. They
say three times a charm. I can feel something lost.
I still care and love her.

"You look bad Elaine. Drinking that vodka all
the time has done a number on you."

"I know I feel terrible.  That is why I wanted
you to come here."

We go onto patio. She lights up a cigarette.

"So you said on the phone the other day you started drinking in the morning. You were crying your heart out."

"I did? I don't remember."

"Wait, you can't remember? That was just yesterday. And that's why I am here to help you."

"I have to go to the restroom."

She leaves. I think to myself, how can she not remember? I shake my head. I wait and wait for her to come back out. Finally I go inside and there she is watching the news like she didn't want to talk anymore.

"I am going to bring to my things."

She does not respond at all.

We sit and watch all her western shows without any conversation.

"I am getting hungry. I am going to fix myself

sandwich. Do you want one?" I said

"Yes."

I look inside her can cabinet.  I see two big boxes of wine and a half gallon of vodka. I come back with tuna sandwich.

"Elaine if you're going to stop drinking you should throw out that wine and vodka."

She doesn't say anything just eats and watches TV like I didn't say anything.

"Elaine don't you want to see my new car?"

"I will after my show."

So she did hear what I said?  I am wondering to myself, did I make another mistake?

Two days go by; no drinking. She is at work.

I am out for a walk.  Things seem okay.  Maybe

this time she really means it. If She cares about us

being together.  I am starting to feel good. Maybe I

will call Wally now.  I should go visit him and

Connie. I walk over to the Walgreen's Shopping Center. I wanted to buy some potato chips for Elaine, she like them. I sit for a minute on a bench in front of the store watching seniors coming and going. All them driving new cars some looking good and some not, health wise. Elaine should be coming home from work by now. So, I hurry back the door patio is open. Did I forget to close it? I look; there she is with a big glass of wine. I just close the patio door.

"Hi, how long have you been home?"

"About an hour. I did all my work and came home."

I wanted to say something about the wine but didn't. Wine was okay and she does work hard, but how many has she had already?

"What have you been up to?"

"Just walking and watching all the seniors."

"What about us seniors?"

"All of them have nice cars and the ladies dress nice; men too.  Sun City is like a new beginning. A world of its own"

She finished that wine then got another one.

Here we go again.  She was getting drunk on wine.

She drinks that one quickly and then gets another one.

"Don't you think you've had enough wine?"

She gave me that look.

"I didn't say I was going to stop drinking wine."

"Over the phone, it sounded like you said all drinking."

"No I didn't say wine and if I want to drink it's my home I can drink whatever I want."

"Why do you think I came here?"

She didn't say anything.  Just finished her drink and went and got another one.  I think she is taking shots of vodka when she is in there.  I feel my blood pressure going up. She came out with big glass of what I thought was vodka.

"It's not vodka, only it water. You want smell it?"
She raises it to me.

"I never put ice in my water."  Her tone was mean and nasty.

It didn't even last a week before she started.

"I am out of here," I said, shaking my head.

"Whatever, I can do what I want. I am 66. Not a teenager to be told what to do."
I pack my two suit cases and leave back to Cottonwood.  I don't say anything and just leave.

That's it.  It's over for good.

She can't stop drinking. She needs help and

she'll never ask for help. Some people like their drinking. But, I don't have to be a part of it.

I feel like Charley Brown when Lucy pulls the ball away about the time he goes to kick it. And he falls for it over and over again. Yes, it would have been nice for both of us to be together in our senior years.

Tears come to my eyes as I drive past Black Canyon City it's a good thing I didn't say anything to Wally and Annie. I can't believe I fell for it again. Is that what love does to you? We all want it so bad. I think we get misled by love, sometimes. I blast the car radio to stop thinking. I wasn't paying attention to my driving. Where am I? I feel torn between love and madness. I pull over trying to get a hold of myself before I ran off the road. I sat there for twenty minutes when a State Trooper goes past heading the other way. He looks at me as if I needed help, so I got back on I 17 headed home.

I get back to Cottonwood and collapse on my sofa. What's wrong with me putting myself through that again? I won't do that again. It is over. My insides are torn up again. It hurts like being shot with a shotgun. I lay on my bed trying to read Florence Henderson's book "Life Is Not a Stage". She had lots of ups and downs. But life is like a stage with all the acts we go through trying to be happy. I am sure God has good life plans for all of us. Things get in the way. We don't think right.

I am not in the right frame of mind to read. I put on ear phones and blast the radio. That works for about half an hour.  I get up and go to Carl's Jr. I decide to have a burger and fries.  I watch all of the people while I am eating.  I bet they have their ups and downs also. Life is no bowl of cherries, that's for sure. All the things I tried and here I sit by myself only wanting to be loved.

Three weeks pass by and I do not hear from Elaine. I am starting to feel like my old self.  I started thinking about doing something with my foundation (Celebration of Youth).  I like working with young people.  They always make you feel good, especially the little ones.  Maybe Gary and I can come up with a fun project for the kids.  I'm finally getting my mind in a positive frame. It is Friday morning my phone starts ringing. I look at the caller ID, it's Elaine.  I am not going to answer it. It is over for us. Several more rings and it stops.

I had a feeling come over me and began to

question myself. Did I do the right thing? It starts

ringing again. I let it ring and ring.  But I can't

ignore it this time.   I answer it.  There is a long

pause.

"Hi, Elaine."
"I stopped drinking."

"What, what did you say?"

"I stopped drinking two weeks ago. I haven't drank anything. I am stopping for good. I can't take it anymore."

"That's great I know you've been talking about stopping smoking, but drinking. That's great I am so happy for you."

"And I may stop smoking too. One thing at a time. Maybe we can get back together soon." she said

"We'll see in time. That would be good for both of us. Let's take it slow. We will just talk on the phone. See how it goes." I said

We talked for hours about all the fun we had doing things together. Going out and just laughing lots. We hung up. I sat there thinking is this for real? Can she really stop drinking? Only time will tell. That would be so great us back together in our senior years just enjoying each other. I look up to God, "Please help her." I said a prayer. Then I called my sister Annie.

"Hi, sis. Guess who I just talked to."

"Elaine?"

"Yes and she said she has stopped drinking everything."

"What? She stopped all by herself? That would be very hard to do, but more power to her if she can stop drinking by herself. But I think she will go back after a while. She needs AA to stop for good. It takes a lot of support. I will say a prayer for her."

"I just hoped it would work out for both of you. Sitting there all day drinking is not good for any one. Sis said "She wants us to be back together"

"I don't know if that will be good for you after your health issues. I know you care for her."

"That's what I am thinking, her drinking and her bad temper.  But if she is ready stopping." we hang up say I love you


Here I sit again thinking, is this for real? Can she really stop drinking? Wally and I did. I have to give her the benefit of the doubt.  She is a strong lady and if it's for us to be together that would mean a lot to me.

If she would stop drinking we could do all those things we talked about. My hopes were up again.  Surprisingly, I felt good with just that little call.  She had been drinking all her life. Now she was going to stop for us.

"Richard take it easy. That's just one phone call!" I said to myself.

She did say that before. Her voice sounded sincere this time. I put my hand together as to pray to God, "Please help her."

It would be great to be back together in our senior years. Here I go again. How your mind works. One moment you're down the next you're up. Life and it surprises. We all want to be loved and give love no matter what age. I'm just trying to be happy. My stomach was reacting. Your whole body reacts to good and bad news. My mind didn't know what to do.

"Just stop it Richard! Go do something. Watch TV." I say to myself.

Instead, I went for a long walk. I'm enjoying all that God had created. There is the big blue

beautiful sky and birds flying by. My spirits were up
again. I couldn't believe how good I felt over that
one call. That would mean so much to me if she
could stop drinking. I almost tried to skip like a kid
but there were other senior couples walking
nearby. I didn't want them to think I had lost it.
That loving feeling always wants to come out in all
of us.

It is there just waiting to make us happy.
That's God's love. We are created in God's image.
I walked all the way to Fry's and then to Jack in the
Box. I had a decaf coffee while I sat and watched
people.

When I get home two hours later there was
a call on my computer magic jack phone from her.
Now it is up to me to help her for both of us. So, I

call her back.

"Hi, you called?"

"Yes. I just wanted to say I really mean what I said and I hope you believe me."

"I do, But, Elaine it won't be that easy. You should go to AA."

Things go silent for a while.
"No, I can quit by myself. But if I can't, maybe I will go to AA"

"Well I am here for you. You know I want us to be together for rest of our senior years. But I can't be around your drinking and your temper. It really affects my blood pressure and it's not good for my health."

"I know that's why I am going to quit drinking. I know I do it by myself."

"One day at a time and lots of prayers I will be saying for you, for us. It will be great to do some of the things we talked about driving the U S A in our camper. Something we both dream of."

"Yes, seeing America together will be special. Maybe take Sugar with us."

We both kind of laughed.

"You know how much I love you and want to be with you."

"Yes and I love you that's why I will do this, stop drinking."
"Let's talk every day and see how it goes. Elaine my heart is with you. Love you."

"Love you, too."
We hang up.  A week passed and we talked

three times a day every day. She sounded so

much better. Like the Elaine I always loved.  She

had stopped drinking. I could tell by the sound of

her voice.  It looked good, us getting back together.

I called my sister and brother telling them how

proud I am of Elaine.  She had stopped stop

drinking and we would be getting back together

soon. Annie was not sure she could stop for good.

It is a battle of the body and heart and the body will

fight for its alcohol, Wally said.  He quit. Maybe she

can too.  Two months pass. We have been talking

all this time, but just small talk such as what we are

going to do, the news, the weather, and personal

things.

We were just getting to know each other better.

Maybe that's what we should have done when we

first starting talking last January.  You can't always

second guest everything.

"Good morning," I say.

"Good morning to you, Mr. Corey. Did you
have a good sleep?"

"Kind of.  I was up at 4:00 a.m.  I had this
weird dream. Sugar was chasing me around your
house. We were having fun."

We both laughed a little

"Why did you wake up?"

"Just had to go to the potty. So, I stayed up and watched a cooking show."

We talked for an hour.

I always said how proud I was of her for stopping her drinking. She said she would save over $100 every month by stopping her smoking and drinking. That is at least $1200 yearly.

"It won't be long and I will be there having my book signing at bell library and I will stay with you. That's going to be so great, us back together." We say our love for each other is stronger than those vices I was feeling real good what year this has been; us finding each other after all those years and me going through a stroke. Only God knows why.

I called my sister. It felt good to talk to her. I told her how proud I was of Elaine. That is she doing this for us but mainly for herself. I was going to stay with her in ten days. Sis said she will say a prayer for her. I was counting the days. It has been months since the last time I was in Sun City. I email Elaine a note to remind her about my book signing at Bell Library. Five day pass; we talk twice a day. It is mostly small talk. I started packing. I was getting excited about seeing her and us trying for the fourth time. Maybe three times a charm for some, but maybe four times is it for us. With her not drinking, things will be great.

We should have a good time just being together and having someone to be with and talk to, planning things in our senior years.

Maybe we wouldn't do all the things we plan, but just sharing our love for each other is what God meant it to be.

It is Saturday after 5:00 p.m. and I call her, but there's no answer. Maybe she went shopping or out walking Sugar.

My computer phone rang. I answered it. It was Elaine.

"Hi, I was out back watering the poinsettia."

"How does it look?" she says.

"Really good. You will be surprised how much it has grown. So what are you doing today? Only one day and I will be there."

"There is something I have to tell you."

"What you're going to have a baby?" I say, jokingly. She doesn't laugh.

"I started drinking and smoking a week ago"

My heart dropped like a ton of bricks. There was a long pause.

"What? Why?"

"It's my home and I can do what I want. I am 66. If I want to drink, I will," she said with a hard tone

"You don't drink for almost three months, but here I am coming to stay with you and you start drinking that damn vodka again? After all those letters I sent you about how I couldn't be around you when you're drinking that hard stuff. You're like a different person. I will only come if you don't drink that vodka."

"It's my home and I will drink what I want."

"Well, I am not coming."
"That's up to you."

I hung up, not saying another word. I sat on

my bed.  I couldn't believe what just happened.

Here we've been talking all those days like

everything was going to be okay. We would be

together. All the history we had. We liked being

together, but then she started drinking. She

couldn't wait and show me that she had stopped

drinking.  I told everyone how proud I was of her

doing this for us.

Tears came to my eyes, I was shaking my head is disbelief. I guess I was just not meant to be happy in this life time. It's over this time. My health and family are more important. All those days hoping this was going to work out and be happy with someone we love for rest of our lives, but only to be bitterly disappointed. I couldn't sleep that night. I was so happy and then that was all destroyed. Days pass and no calls. I had to go to Sun City for a book signing next week. Maybe she will come by and say hi. Perhaps we can still be friends. I remember she said her friend Ann was having birthday that same day. We'll see what happens.

When that day came, I drove by her house

and did my book signing at Bell library, but no

Elaine I guessed that's it for us. I go to my

brother's place to stay that day I tell him and his

girlfriend Connie what happen. That she started

drinking again. That I told her I wouldn't stay with

her. That she it broke my heart again just when am

coming to Sun City. They're in disbelief. Connie is

really sad about whole thing.

"You'd think she want to be happy and change her life in her senior years," Connie said.

"You're better off finding out now. What if you had moved in with her? What a mess that would have been with you selling or giving away all your things in Cottonwood. She doesn't deserve you," Wally said shaking his head.

The rest of the day we had good time visiting.

Connie and Wally have been trying to sell their

house and are having the up and downs with that. I

had very hard time sleep that night. I keep thinking about Elaine. I had lots of nights like that in past years. My brother says take it one day at time. We all say that. But what about those feeling that have come back alive? I guess it's how you look at things. At least I found out I still have those feeling after all those years by myself.  So there's always the good and bad in everything, even love.

It's 6:30 in the morning and I am back on I-17 heading back to Cottonwood trying not to think about Elaine. Why would she do that? She knew I was coming to stay with her and she started drinking?

Maybe she was trying to tell me something. You think of all kinds of things trying to justify life. It can drive you nuts and maybe I was a little nuts believing an alcoholic can stop drinking by themselves. All the pain we go through.

All families have their problems with addictions and there are millions, maybe billions in the world.

I make it to Cottonwood once again. I'm sitting on sofa, hurting inside.

It's hard to be happy when torn apart again and again. All we want is to be happy. Why is it so hard Jesus? I know you died for us, but did it do any good? My stomach wanted food, but I didn't. It's almost noon.

I am half watching the television when my cell phone rings. It's my brother Wally.

"Just called to see if you are okay."

"I am okay, bro. It is just hard to figure things out."

"Maybe you shouldn't. Maybe you need to just let it go. "He said.

"That's not as easy do as it is to say. When you hope things will work out for the good of both of us."

"Well I don't what to say just. I just wanted to be sure you're okay."

"Yes, I' will be okay. As we all say, taking it one day at time. What else is going on?"

"Same old ups and downs trying to sell this home but Connie has her reasons."

"Yes I know."

"Have to go."

"Thanks for calling, love you guys."

"Love you, bro."

We hang up. I start to go fix something to eat. My cell rings again. I thought it was Wally, figured he forgot to tell me something.

"What did you forget?
"Hi."

It was Elaine.

"Sorry I didn't make it to your book signing. I just got your note."

I mailed it a week ago I am thinking.

"How did things go for the book signing?" she continues.

"Okay, I met a nice lady who loves Dobermans. I stayed at stay at Wally's. We had a real nice visit."

I could tell she had been drinking. I did not say anything. The last time we talked she had stopped drinking for a while. I am not sure why, but she began again shortly before I was to come to Sun City for this book signing. When I found out, I told her I would not stay at her house. We just continued with small talk. It was a very strained conversation. No more I love you. Maybe it was over. Maybe we could be phone friends. We continue to call each other for a few more weeks. The conversations are now about television shows we like and the weather.

I make my last call to Elaine. It is 5:00 p.m. She had been drinking. I can tell. It was just small talk at first.

"You know I thought we were going to be together for rest of our senior years. That's why I retired."

"So did I Elaine. I tried. Three times you said you would stop drinking. Then you started again. I was coming to stay with you. It broke my heart. Why would you do that? You know I told you about your drinking and how it change you. How many letters did I send you? You said the same thing about your drinking. Read them again. You know I had a stroke. My blood pressure went sky high when I was around you and your drinking.  Always thinking you would find something to fight about. My health has to come first and my family. I don't want to have another stroke. Maybe this time something worse would happen to me. With all my heart, I wanted us to be together, especially in our senior years. All the great plans we had. If you ever really stop drinking maybe there will still be hope for us. I will always love you as I said before. You're the only lady I every loved.  I have the two rings I showed you. What more can I do?  I even bought a car to come down to Sun City. It is a sad the way things turned out."

All this time she didn't say anything.  She knows in her heart of hearts how I tried.  God bless her and help her.

I LOVE YOU ELAINE

## Writing This Story

I began writing this story after we first started seeing each other again in January of 2015. I love writing, I have been writing for 40 years. Elaine was excited about the idea of our love story as a book. Us back together again after so many years; she was lonely I was lonely. It was clear we still had feelings for each other. When I told her I was going to write this story with all the details, she said go for it. She helped me with the spelling and grammar, because of my dyslexia I am a notoriously bad speller. I am using an editor for the story. There are things that happen in this story that are very personal between Elaine and me. I wrote a love song for us and only us. I am sure Elaine would say something different than what I have written. God knows everything and why everything happened. I do wonder why God brought us together if He knew the outcome. Maybe I was to try to help Elaine stop drinking and she did for a while. She has it in her to stop. Maybe one day she will. It's hard as we all know to beat an addiction. You need help most of the time. God can only do so much. It's a happy and sad story. We had so much going for us; our history, we like being together, liked the same things, we were from the same generation and we both thought we would spend the rest of our senior years together. What more could you ask of life? It goes by so quickly.

Here we are in our golden years just wanting to be happy, in good health and share the rest of our lives with someone we love. Love; they say there is a fine line between love and hate. I hope in my heart that's not what will happen to her die by herself. We are both God's children created in God's love. There is no hate in my heart only hoping one day Elaine will change. Hoping she will get over her problem. I want us to be good friends and maybe see each other once in a while, if nothing more. We are in the same state, less than two hours apart. I would have loved to have written a very, very happy ending.  Everything started out great then things got in the way. Life got in the way.  God bless all of you.  I will take this one day at a time.


Richard E Corey

PS If you're all wondering whether or not I would take Elaine back?

Yes, if she could really stop drinking, I would take her back in a heartbeat.

Not the end???

I am sure, if I dug way back in my memory there would be a whole other story I could write about Elaine and I. How we first met.  How we were crazy in love back in the hippie days of San Francisco; 1969. Maybe I will one day.

Your heart never forgets your first real love does it?

# Acknowledgments

I would like to thank my family and friends for their support in the writing of this book, especially Gary and Lance for their suggestions, advice, and help in making this book a reality.  Seniors tell seniors about this book maybe it will help other seniors with their addictions SENIORS HELPING SENIORS

# GOD BLESS   LOVE TO ALL

## Richard Estrada Corey

This book is dedicated Elaine Ruth Corey and all those who suffer from an addiction.

God Bless all seniors who are going through life changing events.

## About the Author

## Richard E. Corey

Richard was born in Los Angeles, California. The

family moved when he was very young to Yuma,

Arizona, where he spent most of

his young life. Richard attended

and graduated from Yuma High

School and then went on to

attend Western College working on a business

degree. After his short stay in Wester College,

Richard returned to California and took up a

mangers position at a local department store.

From there he moved on to running his own

business; Action Maintenance Products (AMP) an

industrial lighting company. His business serviced

all of Los Angeles for over 7 years.

During this time he still found time to volunteer in a local hospital for mentally challenged youth and adults as well as The Hollywood Hospital assisting AIDS patients as they learned to cope with their condition. Richard decided to end his stint in California after the 1991 riots. This was the time to move on. He moved back to Arizona, Phoenix this time. He took a break from the corporate world. After a few years he moved to Camp Verde, Arizona. A place with a nice, small town feel. Here he opened his own business in furniture restoration and repair. Richard did this for about a year and a half then sold out to move on to bigger and better things. He began working at a local television station. He filmed, edited and produced an assortment of programs focused on community events throughout the Verde Valley.

After watching a KCBS broadcast special hometown meeting about the violence of gangs and drug issues, Richard decided to start his own foundation, The Celebration of Youth Foundation, a non-profit to give the youth a positive avenue towards success. His foundation had lot of support from local and state government and educators. One of his many interests for the last 30 years has been writing. He has written over twelve books. Most books are directed toward the young reader. As they say youth are our future. One book has successfully been self-published on Amazon; Bloodline, The Doberman Family. He has received a lot of great and positive feedback on this book and plans to follow up with several sequels in the years to come.

Richard is now enjoying semi-retirement in Cottonwood, Arizona. We say semi because he is still actively involved in writing and in The Celebration of Youth Foundation. He also has two websites to help support his foundations, artworldofsedonatv.com and petswelovetv.com.

Richard has many other works completed or waiting to be complete.  Most are available on Amazon or Createspace.

**Completed Works:**

The Pinecones That Saved Christmas (DVD)

Abandon

Where are My Friends?

Hear the fire

The Doberman Family Sequel

Cowboy in the Whitehouse & Kicking Butt

Why, Why, Why? The Death of a Child

My Personal Weird Dreams and Sex Dreams Vol 1

My Personal Weird Dreams and Sex Dreams Vol 2

CPSIA information can be obtained
at www.ICGtesting.com
Printed in the USA
LVOW10s1611170118
563093LV00004B/568/P